Acknowledgments

We the editors would like to express a special thanks to Professor Kosuke Shimizu, the Director of Afrasian Research Centre Ryukoku University, who has helped us to bring this volume to completion. We owe a debt of gratitude to Professor Hideaki Sasaki, Ryukoku University, the executive director of the 12th Annual Conference of the Japan Society for Intercultural Studies. The symposium itself was held at the conference co-sponsored by Afrasian Research Centre.

We have been especially fortunate to work with Professor Ryugo Matsui, Ryukoku University, who has given a professional advice to our original planning of this project.

JN176668

"INTERCULTURAL 13" Special International Edition

Editor
The Japan Society for Intercultural Studies
Saya Shiraishi, Chairperson
Ippei Wakabayashi, Editor in Chief

Publisher
Mitsuru Inuzuka
Fukosha Publishing Co., Ltd.

Printing and Bookbinding
Morimoto Printing Co., Ltd.

Foreword

Kosuke SHIMIZU
Director, Afrasian Research Centre
Ryukoku University

There seems to be an increasing interest in the context of the Kyoto School philosophy and global affairs in recent years. This interest is found ubiquitously not only in humanities, but also in such social scientific disciplines as politics, sociology, and international relations (IR). But why Kyoto School now? There seem to be several possible answers to this question. First, there have been a substantial number of books and articles published in international relations theories (IRT) in relation to non-Western discourses. Some non-Western scholars (this does not necessarily mean that they are non-Europeans or non-Americans) focus on international relations the basis of geographical particularity such regions as Africa, Asia, and Latin America or nation-states as China, Korea and India. Therefore it is possible to say that there is an increasing demand from non-Western IRT academia for something particularly Japanese to contribute to IRT diversification.

Another answer is from the discourse of IRT and religion. There have been monographs and papers circulated, which were grounded in Islam and Confucianism, but not much has been written on the ground of Buddhism. This is another reason why we concentrate on Kyoto School in comprehending contemporary world affairs. As many Kyoto School philosophy specialists contend that Nishida Kitaro's philosophy has much in common with Buddhism, it is not surprising that Kyoto School philosophy comes under intensive academic scrutiny.

The last, but not least reason is about the School's political engagement. Infamously, the main members of Kyoto School were involved in the wartime militarist regime during the WWII, and provided justifications for Japan's violent expansion of territory overseas. Why such world-class philosophers agreed to deliver rationalizations for the violent acts of Japan, and what was lying behind their engagement? Out of historicising the Kyoto School philosophy of World History, we can draw a cautionary tale in engaging with the non-Western IRT discourse.

The 12th Conference of the Japan Society for Intercultural Studies in conjunction with the Afrasia Research Centre was held on 6 of July 2013 at the Omiya Campus of Ryukoku University in responding to this growing attention towards the Kyoto School.

The symposium was entitled as 'In Search of Non-Western International Relations Theory: The Kyoto School Revisited'. There are at least two different standing points in understanding of the Kyoto School. One is to comprehend the School as a site of religious philosophy and focus on the philosophy and Buddhism. The other is to draw some political implications from the School's philosophy and this symposium has been mainly conducted by politics and international relations scholars. The 'non-Western' in the symposium's title reflects the concern of the latter, and was to show our particular focus on the relationship between the Kyoto School philosophy and global politics. The Panel was consisted with four presenters: Professor Christian Uhl (Ghent University), Dr. Satofumi Kawamura (Research Fellow, Center for Philosophy, The University of Tokyo), Professor Chih-yu Shih (National Taiwan University), and Kosuke Shimizu (Afrasian Research Centre, Ryukoku University).

Prof. Uh is one of the most critical Japan studies specialists in Europe with a particular focus on politics and religion, and have numerous publications in English and German. He is currently working at the Ghent University, and also a member of Ghent Centre for Buddhist Studies. As he has been working on Buddhism and politics of Japan and China, it seems to be natural that he started focusing on the Kyoto School. Prof. Uhl presented a paper titled "Nishida's Logic, and the Notion of the Nation: A Footnote to a Remark by Karatani Kōjin Concerning a Leibniz Syndrome in 20th Century Political Thought" in which he casts a new light on Nishida's 'New World Order' article in compering another great scholar of the continental philosopher of rationalism, Leibniz.

Dr. Kawamura deliver a presentation entitled "Tekhnē, Culture and New Order: Elimination of Politics by Nishida Kitarō", and argued that Nishida's war involvement was not to glorify the expansionist policies of the dominant regime of the time. However, as Nishida tried to hide and repress the political dimension in his philosophy, he lost the critical perception towards the prevailing order.

Followoing Dr. Kawamura's provocative presentation, Prof. Chih-yu Shih of National Taiwan University, showed his attention to Kyoto School in terms of international political theory (IRT). His concern was with how to understand East Asian identities under the Western hegemony of universalised IRT. Such countries in East Asia as Taiwan, China and Japan, are often seen by the Western observers to be ambiguous because of the in-betweenness of their identities. The place of nothingness of the Kyoto School provides a viewpoint to explicate their ambiguity for further clarification.

The last was Kosuke Shimizu, the director of Afrasian Research Centre of Ryukoku University. I tried in this paper to address the relationship between the Kyoto School's involvement with the militarist regime of Japan in the WWII and contemporary non-Western IRT discourses. I argued that there are some striking similarities between them, and we can draw a cautionary tale from the history of the Kyoto School philosophy.

These papers differ from each other in their theoretical scope, perspectives, analytical methodology, and reasons for taking up the School's philosophy. However, they have one thing in common, that is, they all see the School having a tremendous possibility in furthering the research of contemporary world affairs. I, and surely all of participants in the panel, wish more research to be conducted in order to utilize the School's unprecedented wisdom.

[Symposium]
On Nishida Kitarō's "Leibnizian" Logic, and his Notion of the Nation

Christian UHL
Ghent University

In this paper, I present some preliminary reconsiderations on the interconnection between Nishida Kitarō's later logic and his political philosophy. These reconsiderations will form the core of an essay in which I intend to use Karatani Kōjin's remarks concerning a certain "Leibniz-syndrome" in twentieth-century political thought as a starting point for a more in-depth inquiry into Nishida's philosophy, as an expression of the contradictions and aporias of global capitalist modernity. At the present stage of my project, at which I am still struggling with analyzing my primary sources, I cannot do adequate justice to the existing research and confine myself to an attempt at organizing my preliminary notes on some of the basic primary texts into a readable form (if not otherwise indicated, all translations are by the author).

*

Karatani Kōjin (1994), in the first chapter, "Teikoku to nēshon" (Empire and Nation) of his book, "*Senzen*" *no shikō* ("Pre-War" Thinking), discusses the tensions, contradictions, and aporias within the established notions of national and transnational "imagined communities." Later in this chapter, Karatani speaks about the significance of Luther's translation of the Bible into the German vernacular and the subsequent reform of religion (such as the individualization of belief and the dissolution of transcendence by means of the privacy of inner language) in the emergence of a German national consciousness. In this context, Karatani also introduces Leibniz as a thinker, who, as Karatani points out, is known for his monadology and for his attempt at creating a universal sign language of logics. However, as Karatani remarks, these inventions were not merely philosophical endeavors, but have to be also regarded in relation to the attempt to form a logic capable of recreating European unity consequent to its disintegration caused by the religious schism. The monad, as Karatani writes, which mirrors the whole, is the image of a unity, within which "each monad (individual) is neither merely isolated, nor integrated into the whole in a totalitarian way" (Karatani 1994, 18–9). One can discover such a logic of a "soft empire" in the EU today, but it also existed in the 1930s, for example, in the writings of Paul Valery, or, last but not least, in the political philosophy of Nishida Kitarō. Karatani quotes a lengthy passage from the latter's "Principle of the New World Order" (1945), which I condense slightly as follows:

> "... [T]he fall of the world into [a state of] fierce struggle was just inevitable. This is the case, because today, due to the advance of science, technology and economy, each state-building nation (*kokka minzoku*, Nishida's rendering of the German word, '*Staatsvolk*') has entered one single and tight global space. The only solution here is that each of them awakens to its global mission, that each of them remains in strict conformity with itself, and yet transcends itself and contributes to the formation of one global world. ... Saying that each state-building nation transcends itself and contributes to the constitution of one world has nothing in common with any so called national autonomism such as that of Wilson's League of Nations, according to which all nations are simply equal and recognize each other's independence. That kind of world does not transcend the narrow horizon of the abstract world ideal of the 18th century. The current world war is proof enough of the fact that with this ideal, it is impossible to meet the requirements of the present day. Each state-building nation has grown out of its distinct historical ground and has its distinct world-historical mission, and therefore, each of them has a particular historical life. That all state-building nations ... constitute one global world can only mean that each of them transcends itself by first constituting a particular world of its own in accordance with its local traditions, and that then, due to the unification of these particular worlds, ... the whole world as one global world [i.e., as a world of worlds] comes into existence. ... This is the ultimate ideal

of the historical development of humankind, and this ideal has to be the principle as well of the new world order the current war is calling upon us. Our country's ideal, as it has manifested itself in the words, the whole world under a single roof (*hakkō ichiu*), must have a similar meaning." (Karatani 1994, 20-1; Nishida 1978-80a, 430)

In the context of wartime Japan, as Karatani points out, Nishida's notion of a "world of worlds" was not more than an exegesis of the ideology of Japanese imperialism. However, and regardless of its strong Hegelian taste, Nishida's "Principle of the New World Order" is, at the same time, yet another manifestation of the Leibnizian ideal of a "soft empire," as Karatani writes, before he concludes, "The Leibnizian model, as a 'form', is always effective. Philosophically, as Althusser has pointed out, this is the case because this form as such does not have any meaning of its own. In this respect, any future philosophical signification of such a 'community' too can arguably only be a Leibnizian one. This applies already to the European Union, and a similar logic will be probably proposed in the case of the formation of an economic union of East Asia" (Karatani 1994, 21-2).

*

Thus, Karatani, after having read into Leibniz's logics a certain political intention, applies a reverse strategy when he divides Nishida's "Principle" into an explicit political content and an implicit general logical form, which he then *qua* homology identifies as Leibnizian. Let us move away from discussing Karatani at this point and attempt a substantiation of his useful, yet vague, hint by further distilling this logical "essence" from Nishida's earlier essay, "The Self-Identity and Continuity of the World" (1936); there, Nishida writes as follows:

"If the many does exist, then there must be individual, independent things. If these are one, then they cannot be independent and individual. That the many is the one is a contradiction …. If something does exist, which as a real contradictory unity is identical with itself, then the individual has to be individual through and through, and the whole has to wholly be the whole. That the individual is individual through and through means that it determines itself and is not determined by others. That the whole is wholly the whole means that it encompasses and determines the individual beings, or at least that it mediates individuals with each other …. In any case, continuity has to be thought of as the unity of the contradiction between the individual, independent things, and the universal, it has to be thought of as the self-identity of absolute contradictory things …. In particular, Hegel's dialectics have to be something like this." (Nishida 1978-80b, 7-8)

These lines highlight the difficulties Nishida faces in formulating a view that integrates the multitude *vis-à-vis* the unity of the world. These difficulties result from the interplay of two axiomatic presumptions: on the one hand, the presumption that there are individual things, which, as such, might seem to be rather unproblematic and evident, or, at the least, in accordance with our everyday experience; and, on the other hand, the presumption that, nevertheless, this fragmented and manifold reality is in fact a unity, and thus one. Under this second presumption of the unity and oneness of the world — which is not evident at all — the status of the individual becomes a problem. The unity and oneness of reality was Nishida's point of departure in his first book, *Inquiries into the Good* (1911), where he tried to grasp what he calls "true reality" by means of his concepts of "immediate," "pure," and "religious experience." However, the fact that allows us to distinguish the above quotation from Nishida's earlier writings, in a study of of his later philosophy, is that in the quotation, Nishida tries his luck with dialectics (a fact that is not apparent to the readers of his "Principle of the New World Order"). This shift toward dialectics might indicate his growing (and in a certain way more "this-worldly") concern with the status of the individual *vis-à-vis* the universal, and thus, a more problematic understanding of the relationship between the two, so that we should consider specifying our rendering of Nishida's question: how to logically and conceptually integrate the multitude *vis-à-vis* the unity of the world, in a way that is, however, not hierarchical and allows him to defend the status of the particular against the totalizing claims of the universal. This phrasing, indeed, puts a certain limit on the extent to which one can expect Nishida to have been a proponent of any empire, (even if it were a "soft" one) rather than a nationalist (or better still: perhaps he was a proponent of a "soft empire" precisely *because* he was a nationalist). Moreover, Nishida's explicit reference to Hegel's dialectics also limits the extent to which one can expect his logics to be really Leibnizian. Thus, let us examine the details more closely.

*

When Nishida discusses the question of what the individual actually is, then his reasoning occasionally oscillates between two thinkers: Aristotle and Leibniz. "I always think," as Nishida writes, "that the one who defined the individual logically for the first time was, as a matter of fact, Aristotle. Leibniz's definition of the individual too is, undoubtedly, based on the Aristotelian one" (Nishida 1978–80c, 69–70). Thus, let me start with Aristotle, and then move on to Leibniz.

Aristotle's name for the individual thing, "*hypokaimenon*," means "the underlying," that is, the "base," or in other words, that what is "at the root." In his *Metaphysics*, he explains, "The *hypokaimenon* is that thing, of which all the rest is said, but which itself is not predicating something else." According to Aristotle, the *hypokaimenon* is distinguished from the accidents, that is, the predicates attributed to it or its general properties, because it is the cause of these accidents, because, in contrast to these, it is an individual thing, and as such an individual thing, it is "separate" and "independent." The *hypokaimenon*, accordingly, is the individual thing as the "first essence"; logically speaking, it is the last subject of everything that can be predicated, and, ontologically speaking, it is the substance, that is, an independent being, which "carries" the secondary, accidental being and, in this sense, is "underlying" it (Aristotle 1991, 9; 376–77).

Let us examine Aristotle's definition: if something universal (the predicate) is said about something individual — for example, "Aristotle was a teacher of Alexander the Great," or "Aristotle was a human being," or "A human being is a living being" — it means that the complete notion of the individual would result from the sum of all predicates that can possibly be attributed to it. However, a problem occurs here in that however many predicates one attributes, it seems as if, according to Aristotle's own definition, the individual always has to remain separate from, and beyond, its own properties, and, thus, can never be reached by means of predication. Aristotle's logic relates all predicates to the *hypokaimenon*, but the *hypokaimenon* as such seems to always remain in the dark beyond the horizon of predication, or, in other words, of language and thinking. Seen from this perspective of predication, it appears to be a kind of irrational leftover, and here, Nishida steps in; he concludes that Aristotle's individual is a threshold value: "Aristotle's individual is just something that has been defined right up to the utmost limit of the abstract universal" (Nishida 1978-80d, 212). In this sense — that is to say, because the "individual, which is always the subject and never becomes a predicate must be that what transcended the abstract universal" (Nishida 1978-80e, 356)" — Nishida speaks of the individual also as the "transcendental subject."

So far, so good. Yet, Aristotle's *hypokaimenon* poses a problem not only with regard to the limits of predication, but also with regard to the status of the individual *vis-à-vis* the universals (the predicates). According to Aristotle, the individual is subsumed in the universals, and, therefore, the independence that Aristotle's definition grants the individual in the first place is canceled out. If the individual shall be really independent and identical with itself, then it must be regarded as a thing that determines itself, or, in other words, it has to possess or contain within itself all the predicates that can possibly be attributed to it — and precisely at this point, Nishida brings Leibniz into play as follows: "Leibniz argues that it is not sufficient to define the individual by saying that it is the subject and never becomes a predicate. All predicates must be contained within the subject. That what can be thought of as something that causes everything that ever happens to it by itself and to which nothing ever happens because of something else, *that* is an individual" (Nishida 1978-80c, 70). However, how can one possibly agree with this objection against Aristotle right after one has defined the individual as a "transcendental subject"? At this point, our exercise becomes somewhat complicated. In order to determine precisely where our problem lies, we should have a closer look at Leibniz's views.

*

We saw that Karatani considered Leibniz to be the thinker who, besides his monadology, is known for a project that Leibniz himself described as follows: "If one could find characters and symbols, which are capable of expressing our thoughts as purely and as strictly as arithmetic expresses the numbers, or analytical geometry, the lines, then one obviously should be able to do with regard to all subjects, which are subject to reason, what one does in arithmetic and geometry" (Leibniz 1999a, 6); Leibniz writes elsewhere, "every mistake of the calculus proves itself to be a mistake of thinking" (Leibniz 2000, 19). Karatani, as we have seen, regards this project as being driven also by the wish to restore European unity. In the first place, however, Leibniz's project is driven by the very baroque intention to discover the language of a *scientia universalis*, namely, the universal language of calculating reason. As a result of this effort, Leibniz invented the logical calculus, the elements and combinations of which are represented by symbols, which stand only for themselves and do not signify anything else. Hence, the calculus "is valid not only for numbers and quantities, but also for other things" (Leibniz 1960, 68), such as, for example, the law of identity:

$$A=A$$

If we interpret the letters of the calculus as numbers and quantities, then we have math; yet, if interpreted as concepts, then the calculus can also express, for example, Aristotelian syllogistics.

Leibniz's disagreement with Aristotle, as underscored by Nishida in the aforementioned quotation, lies with the fact that concepts can be interpreted in two different ways, namely, either with regard to their *extent*, or with regard to their *intent*. Let us take, for example, the sentence (cf. Schupp 2003, 244-5): "All human beings are living beings." In extensional interpretation, this means that all individuals, who come under the concept "human being," are contained in the group of individuals, which comes under the more encompassing concept, "living being." From the intentional point of view, however, a being, which is not a living being in the first place, can — impossibly — qualify as a human being. However, to be a living being is a prerequisite to being a human being. Thus, in intentional interpretation, the same sentence would rather mean that, by contrast, the concept of the "human being" always encompasses or "includes" that of the "living being." Traditional, as well as modern, logics are biased in favor of the extensional point of view (ibid.). The logic of Leibniz is one of the exceptions, as the following passage from his *Discourse de métaphysique* might illustrate (this passage has probably informed Nishida's aforementioned statement).

"If several predicates can be attributed to one and the same subject, and if this subject itself is not a predicate of anything else, then it is probably correct to call this subject an individual substance; but this is not sufficient, such an explanation is just an explanation of the word. Accordingly, one has to consider what it means that something can truly be attributed to a certain subject. As a matter of fact, every true judgment is grounded in the nature of things, and if a sentence is not identical, that is, if the predicate is not explicitly included in the subject, then it has to be at the least virtually included in it." (Leibniz 1991, 17)

Therefore, as Leibniz continues, the subject always has to include the predicate, so that somebody, who comprehends the subject completely, could also decide if a certain predicate can be attributed to it or not. Accordingly, the "essence of a complete substance, or subject, respectively, consists in a concept so complete that it would be possible to comprehend and deduce from it all the predicates of the subject to which this concept belongs" (ibid., 17-8). In other words, Leibniz does not distinguish between necessary judgments such as "the sum of the angles of the triangle is 180°" and a contingent one such as "Aristotle was the teacher of Alexander the Great." Indeed, a limited line of argumentation would suffice in order to prove the law of Pythagoras, whereas the line of argumentation would have to be endless in the case of a contingent statement. The difference, however, is not a fundamental one, as Leibniz would argue, but one that simply derives from the limitations of our cognitive faculties (cf. Schupp 2003, 252):

"If, on the other hand, God conceives the individual concept [...] of Alexander, then He would see therein at the same time the ground of, and the cause for, all predicates that really can be attributed to him — for example, that he will conquer Darius and Porus; He would even know *a priori* (and not only from experience), if he died a natural death or by poison, which we can only know from history. And if we consider properly how everything is related, then one can say, that in Alexander's soul are always repercussions of everything which will ever happen to him, and even traces of each and everything that ever takes place in the universe." (Leibniz 1991, 18).

Leibniz's name for such an individual substance is "monad." The monad is considered to be indivisible, and thus, has to have no extension. Since a monad has no extension, it must be disembodied and spiritual. Moreover, as an absolute, independent substance, it is "windowless," that is to say, no determination can emerge from, or enter into, a monad. Monads, nevertheless, are in a permanent process of change, driven by an inner urge to achieve completeness (cf. Leibniz 1982a, 27-31). In this process, each monad experiences the restrictions imposed on it by all the others, and thus, perceives its relation to them like a geometrical point at which countless angles converge. That a monad is "windowless" but, nevertheless, related to all others and "knows" their states, means, as Leibnitz writes, "that every monad is a living mirror, which is capable of inner activity, reflects the universe from its own point of view, and is organized in the same way as the universe" (Leibniz 1982b, 5). This universe, that is, the world as a whole, is like a puzzle composed of only monads, and thus far, the formal resemblance between this puzzle and Nishida's above notion of the nations as "distinct worlds of their own," which are "in strict conformity with themselves" and yet constitute a "global world" (cf. the above quotation from Nishida's "Principle of the New World Order"), is, indeed, quite striking. I say "thus far" since we still have to add dialectics to the picture.

*

Nishida's interest in Leibniz developed in the 1920s, and subsequently, he refers frequently to the latter. Eventually, Nishida referred to his own philosophy as a "dialectical monadology" (cf. for example, Nishida 1979-80d, 96); and perhaps, it was his study of Leibniz's works that also motivated Nishida to append "graphical explanations" to a couple of his later philosophical essays. Leibniz occasionally illustrated his own logical considerations by means of the so-called "Eulerian circles" (*Eulersche Kreise*), and we can find something similar in Nishida's collections of philosophical essays as well. The following graph is a more complex example of such graphical explanations (Nishida 1978-80fn, 221):
At first glance, instead of enhancing our understanding of the matter in question, this illustration might be rather discouraging. However, it presents this whole matter in a compact form, and its main elements

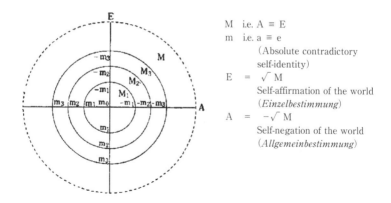

M i.e. A ≡ E
m i.e. a ≡ e
  (Absolute contradictory
  self-identity)
E = √ M
  Self-affirmation of the world
  (*Einzelbestimmung*)
A = −√ M
  Self-negation of the world
  (*Allgemeinbestimmung*)

will be discussed in the following pages. Let us start with Nishida's own explanation of the graph:

> "In light of the above graph, for the first time a world becomes thinkable in which the independent individuals affect each other. A world of individual beings [m, arguably for monad] affecting each other must have this logical structure. This is what I call a "dialectical universal." Whatever kind of real world [$M_{1, 2, 3, ...}$] we may conceive of, we always have to think of it as being an aspect of the dialectical world [M]. This world is... the world of historical reality. This world ... has its poles in the direction of self-determination of the individual, E, as well as in the direction of self-determination of the universal, A." (Ibid.)

This explanation of Nishida's graph can be read as a paraphrase of the above quote on page three of this paper: "If something does exist, which as a real contradictory unity is identical with itself, then the individual has to be individual through and through, and the whole has to wholly be the whole ... it has to be thought of as the self-identity of absolute contradictory things," and so on. In light of such statements, however, it is obvious that Nishida, when designating his own philosophy as a "dialectical monadology," not only expresses his intellectual indebtedness to Leibniz, but underscores, at the same time, the difference between his point of view and that of Leibniz. First, Nishida's world, in which everything real is a coincidence of the two contradictory principles of the "self-determination of the individual" (in the illustration, E, from *Einzelbestimmung*) on the one hand and the "self-determination of the universal" (A, from *Allgemeinbestimmung*) on the other, seems to be fundamentally at odds with Leibniz's concept of truth, according to which "we assess everything as false, which contains a contradiction, and as true everything, which is opposed to falsehood, that is, to that, which is contradictory" (Leibniz 1982a, 41). This is one of Leibniz's renderings of Aristotle's law of non-contradiction.

Leibniz's interpretation of the law of non-contradiction is mainly concerned with the relation between subject and predicate in a proposition, and in this respect, it is different from the classical Aristotelian one; however, this difference is not of interest to us. At this point, three things are important: (i) that the law of non-contradiction presupposes a strict ontological dualism (such as subject and predicate and self and other); (ii) that the law of non-contradiction is a derivative of the law of identity ($A = A$); and, last but not least, (iii) that this law is the essence of Leibniz's monadology (and the ultimate reason why the monads have to be "windowless"). According to Leibniz, identity is the identity of the indistinguishable, or, in other words, the indistinguishableness of the identical, and hence, two otherwise completely identical things are still two distinct things and therefore not identical. Identity, thus, is always self-identity, in the strict tautological sense of the expression $A = A$. Hegel, a seasoned dialectition, held the following view about identity, as expressed in the following remark he added to arguably the most famous chapter of his *Greater Logic*:

> "In this remark, I will have a closer look at identity as the *law of identity*, which is commonly referred to as the most fundamental law of thinking. This law in its positive expression, $A = A$, is, first of all, not more than the expression of the void *tautology*. Therefore, it has been rightly stated that this law of thinking is *without content* and does not get us any further. Thus, it is the void identity, to which those adhere, who, as such, take it as something true, and who always claim that the identity is not the difference, but that identity and difference are different. They don't realize that they, already by claiming this, say that identity is something different ..." (Hegel 1969, 41).

Leibniz is one of those, and accordingly, seen from a Leibnizian point of view, such a thing as a "*dialectical* monadology" is by itself a contradiction in terms, and, arguably, as nonsensical as a Zen-Buddhist *kōan*. Of course, Nishida did not regard himself as an "anti-Leibnizian". Otherwise, he would not have called his own philosophy a "dialectical *monadology*"; and yet, not only does he not hesitate to call his monadology "dialectical," he also does so with an explicit reference to Hegel: "Leibniz's world of pre-established harmony must be Hegel's world of the dynamic idea" (Nishida 1978–80c, 94).

*

The problem that Leibniz's model poses for Nishida is the fact that it allows for the monadic independence of individuals, but not for any real interaction or "co-operation" between them. As windowless as monads are, they are capable of an "inner activity," but not of really "affecting each other," as required by Nishida's aforementioned graphical explanation. Leibniz's monads, as Nishida writes, "are merely intellectual and therefore have no effects. But something which has no effect is not a real individual" (ibid., 101). Kant points this out in criticizing Leibniz's rationalist lack of empirical sense as follows:

> "Leibniz's monadology has no other reason, than that this philosopher thought of the difference between inside and outside only in relation to the intellect. The substances as such must have something *internal* [*etwas Inneres*], which is free from all external circumstances, and, accordingly, also from composition. Thus, the one-fold, singular, uncomplex [*das Einfache*] is the basis of the interior of the things as they are. The interior of their condition [*das Innere ihres Zustandes*], however, cannot be position, shape, contact, or movement either (because all of these determinations are external relations), and so, we can attribute to the substances no other inner condition than that by which we determine our own purpose [*Sinn*] internally, namely, the *condition of the perceptions* [*Vorstellungen*]. This way, the monads were made up, which are supposed to be the elements out of which the universe is built, but the active power of which consist only in perceptions, so that they are effective only within themselves. For the

same reason, however, his principium of the possible community of the substances could have only been a pre-established harmony, and not any physical influence…." (Kant 1968, 295)

The term "pre-established harmony" is Leibniz's answer to the question of understanding how and why the "windowless" monads can serve (like the stones of a mosaic) as the building blocks of the world as a whole, and in his *Theodizee*, Leibniz defends this mosaic as chosen by God as the best of all possible worlds (see also 1982a, 51-3). Nishida's "dialectical universal," on the other hand, is supposed to exist without such an intervention from God. In contrast to Leibniz's world, Nishida's "dialectical universal" is meant to be "not a world of pre-established harmony, but a world that creates itself," and in this respect, he also distinguishes his "dialectical monadology" from that of Leibniz's by calling his own a "creative" (*sōzōteki*) one (Nishida 1978-80c, 96; 97). I wonder, however, if Nishida does justice to Leibniz, whose God, arguably, is not much more than a concession to his contemporaries' expectations. Often enough, Leibniz does not seem to require God at all, but contents himself with an almost Darwinist "metaphysical mechanism" owing to which only the strongest and fittest of everything that is possible becomes real: "From here, one can perfectly understand in which way a divine mathematics or a metaphysical mechanism is at work …. In this way, a world emerges, which gives rise to the most ample production of what is possible" (Leibniz 1966, 42-3). Indeed, as a "metaphysical mechanism," or a "divine mathematics," God has almost completely dissolved into pure abstraction and is needed only as a sufficient reason as to why there is something in the first place and not just nothing (cf. Schupp 2003, 259). The *principium rationis sufficientis* is yet another inalienable article of the rationalist creed, and since God can serve as a sufficient reason for practically everything, other rationalists eventually came up with some proof for the existence of God (cf. ibid., 260). God — or "divine mathematics" — is the mortar, so to speak, that keeps the stones of Leibniz's monadic mosaic together and in place, without really being part of the mosaic.

In Nishida's aforementioned graph, we find a broken line in place of God. It represents the "universal of all universals" (the extensional "pole" of Nishida's world), which is always predicate and never becomes a subject. Since it never becomes subject to any predication, it remains as transcendent to predication as the already mentioned "transcendental subject" (the intentional "pole" of Nishida's world), and accordingly, Nishida also calls it the "transcendental predicate." As the "universal of all universals," which contains all other universals and, thus, can never be contained itself, it must be vast and empty in an absolute sense (cf. for example, Nishida 1979–80g, especially 272–89). Therefore, Nishida, in a certain period of the unfolding of his philosophy, also spoke of it as an "absolute nothingness" and occasionally insinuated a connection between this concept and certain Buddhist ideas. He even promoted it as a unique contribution of the "East" to the "Western" tradition of philosophy, which, as he declared, conceived of the world from the standpoint of "Being" instead (cf. Nishida 1979–80h, 429–30). The nimbus of a putative "Eastern-ness" of Nishida's philosophy has met, and still meets, the expectations and desires of many of his readers, who stare more or less exclusively into the abyss of this "Eastern nothingness," forgetting, not only that its putative Eastern-ness was invented on the stage of global modernity, but also that this nothingness is only one of two "poles" in between which Nishida's world "creates itself" (see the above graph). Nishida's main concern is this real, auto-poetical "world of individual beings affecting each other." As the "transcendental subject" that is not more than an infinitesimal point, and as real as the zero in the center of Nishida's graph, the infinite "universal of all universals" too, is a limit value. It is not part of the "real world," and hence, in Nishida's graph, its horizon is marked not by another continuous line but merely by a broken one. Similar to the other pole of the "transcendental subject," language and reason can approach it asymptotically but never reach it, and thus, it can be postulated but never known objectively. For this reason, one might feel tempted to see in Nishida an anti-rationalist. Yet, as Nishida argues, reason itself dictates the postulation of this other pole, so that between the two of them, the logical matrix can unfold itself, in which everything real, including language and reason, must be logically "rooted" (cf. the graph, $\sqrt{}$, $-\sqrt{}$). Thus, this other pole, which is as empty and abstract as Leibniz's "divine mathematics," is Nishida's logical *conditio sine qua non* and his sufficient reason, and hence, one might argue that Nishida was perhaps not as much of an anti-rationalist as I have just insinuated. Perhaps, he was both romantic and rationalist at the same time and, thus, as self-contradictory as the term "dialectical monadology."

*

I have highlighted how far Nishida's "monadology," which according to Nishida himself is rather "like Hegel's dialectics," is at odds with Leibniz's monadology. However, this is just one side of the problem. We also have to understand how far Nishida's "dialectical monadology," as a "monadology," is at odds with Hegel's dialectics. In fact, Nishida, who on the one hand criticizes Leibniz's monadological incapability to grasp the world "dialectically," on the other hand criticizes Hegel's dialectics and argues "monadologically" that in light of Hegel's logic "the true individual is inconceivable" (Nishida 19978-80i, 447). Hegel's notion of the "identity of the identical and the non-identical" overcomes the dualism of A and non-A. Yet, Hegel presumes *knowledge* as the absolute (the "absolute idea" of Hegel's *Logic*), the unfolding of which is governed by a strict teleology, which does not allow for grasping the relation of the many and the one in any other way than that of a logical subsumption of the former into the latter. Hegel, as Adorno complains, "presupposes from the start positivity as all-comprehensibility," and in the end "he rakes in the prey of the primacy of logics over the meta-logical" (Adorno 1997, 162); such a standpoint of positivity, of Being, as Nishida points out, "does not represent the logic of the real historical world" (Nishida 1978-80i, 447) either. In contrast to Hegel's system, Nishida's "historical world" is designed as an open, infinite, a-genetic, and a-teleological "place" (*basho*), which allows the individual beings, just as they are, to relate to each other by contradicting each other. "A and B exist independently *from each other*," as Nishida points out (emphasis added), and he continues, "therefore, correctly speaking, neither does A exist due to A itself, nor B due to B itself. A and B do not exist without being related to each other. A exists due to the fact that it is in opposition to B, and B exists due to the fact that it is in opposition to A" (Nishida 1978-80b, 88). We can probably translate this statement of Nishida into the following formula, thereby using one of the symbols in the legend to Nishida's aforementioned "graphical explanation:

$$(A = A) \equiv (B = B)$$

I could have used the symbol $\leftrightarrow$ instead of $\equiv$, but in the above graph, Nishida uses the latter. In propositional logics, both symbols signify a so-called material equivalence and have to be read as "if, and only if"; hence, the calculus reads "A is A, if, and only if B is B (and vice versa)." I think this formula makes it easier to grasp Nishida's objective. He sides with Hegel to overcome the Leibnizian model, according to which A = A, and B = B, and the only possible relation between the two is that of a prefab harmony, fixed and determined by the intervention of an artificial, rationalist *deus ex machina*. Yet, on the other hand, he sides with Leibniz, to prevent his "dialectics" from taking off and forsaking the independence and self-identity of the individual. A and B relate to, and "affirm" each other, and they constitute and "affirm" the "world" by contradicting or "negating" each other and the "world"; they contradict each other and the "world" precisely *because* they are independent and self-identical individuals, and they are independent and self-identical individuals precisely *because* they contradict each other and the "world." Thus, Nishida's "world" is not dialectical in the strict sense, but rather a sort of *coincidentia oppositorum*, which does not overcome, but rather confirms and emphasizes the difference of identity and difference and the abovementioned implications of the law of contradiction, namely, the ontological dualism of subject and predicate and self and other, among others. "Each monad" as Nishida writes, "originates itself by expressing itself; and yet, it expresses itself by negating itself and expressing the world. The monads are thus co-originating, and form the world's perspectives; they form the world interexpressively through their own mutual negation and affirmation" (Nishida 1887, 58).

*

Nishida's point of view poses several philosophical problems that need to be addressed urgently. Yet, I think we have done enough work to follow Nishida on his descent from the wintry plateau of logical abstraction down into the depressions of political philosophy. These depressions, we should remind ourselves, were particularly depressing at a time when the modern capitalist Japanese state, like fascist Germany or Italy, externalized its internal economic and social contradictions and conflicts ideologically by presenting itself as a young, global revolutionary, facing the unjust and out-dated world order of the old, "bourgeois" Anglo-American capitalist democracies. Accordingly, many intellectuals embraced the war as healthy refreshment for an allegedly decadent, disintegrating modern Japanese society. This, in summary, is the context of Nishida's above quoted "Principles of the New World Order."

Nishida's frequent use of the word "self-negation" may raise the expectation that any political order that he could possibly have envisioned must be one based on selfless mutual "affirmation" and respect, as harmonious and peaceful as life in a Zen-Buddhist monastery. Yet, in light of the work we have done so far, it should not surprise us too much that such expectations do not materialize. They actually evaporate completely in light of statements such as the following passage from a text in which Nishida, for the first time, uses Tanabe Hajime's term "species" (*shu*), which in Nishida's later writings, serves as the *terminus technicus* for "*minzoku*" or People (in the sense of the German word, *Volk*), emphasizing "*gemainshafto*" or community (German: *Gemeinschaft*) as opposed to "*shakai*," society. Nishida writes as follows:

> "What I call world is not an abstract, universal world of world citizens. To become individual (*koseiteki*) does not mean to become an individual person (*kojinteki*). Reality is in every respect determined, and yet, historical reality exists where the self contains within itself self-negation, and transcends itself, and goes from [one] reality to [another] reality, and this can only mean that in every respect a species asserts itself from its own standpoint as a species, and that within the same environment multiple species oppose each other and struggle with each other. This is what I call the world of historical reality. The world is a place of contradictory self-identity, where the one is the many, and the many is the one. For this reason, I understand the present day, which is commonly regarded as the most nationalist period of history, as the most international one. Never before was there a period as real as our own. Because the world is real, every country has to be nationalist. Today, the world is not outside of the country, but inside of it. To say that the world is just outside is like saying that there is no world at all. Once, Rome's conquest turned Europe into a singular world. Today, one can say that British capitalism has turned the world into a singular world. To become individual (*koseiteki*) does not mean to become particular (*tokushuteki*). It means to become, in historical reality, a bearer of the

times. This, however, does not mean to lose one's particularity, but to make one's particularity truly particular, that is, to become a living species. One can think of the particular as the concrete, but something truly concrete and particular must embrace self-negation, that is to say, it has to be individual (*koseiteki*). Individuality is a quality, which only those have who determine themselves dialectically, it is the power of living beings. As long as one merely faces other, unrelated persons as intellectual objects (*chiteki taisho*), then individuality too is not more than just an object of understanding (*ryōkai no taisho*). Yet, individuality is a power, which is at work within the self. One may regard the self as being merely speculative (*shiiteki*), but, in any case, it is the formative function (*keisei sayō*), which is at work within the historical, corporeal self." (Nishida 1978-80j, 519-20).

I have quoted at length because I think that this passage serves as a stable bridge between our previous analysis of Nishida's "dialectical monadology" and his initially quoted "Principles of the New World Order." First, Nishida's distinction between a merely abstract, merely "intellectual" individuality on the one hand and the true individuality of a "living species" on the other clearly resonates with his previous critique of Leibniz's monads as being "merely intellectual" and therefore having "no effects." This distinction also underpins Nishida's critique at the beginning of this passage of the notion of an "abstract, universal world of world citizens," which, again, resonates with his critique in his "Principles" of Wilson's League of Nations, "according to which all nations are simply equal and recognize each other's independence. That kind of world does not transcend the narrow horizon of the abstract world ideal of the eighteenth century," namely, the horizon of rationalism and of the Enlightenment. Furthermore, we can clearly understand here what "self-negation" and "affirmation" of the other really mean, namely, to end one's eighteenth century style "windowless" existence, to crack one's shell, to go out, and to become a true "historical, corporeal self" by engaging and grappling with the real world, which is a dialectical battlefield, on which "species and species don't connect immediately. Between them there is always only struggle (*tōsō*)... The historical world as contradictory self-identity is a world of struggle (*tōsō no sekai*), in which species and species wrestle with each other for ever," as Nishida confirms (1978-80k, 320). In addition, elsewhere he writes, "Heraklitus says that opposite things unite, that from difference, the most beautiful harmony arises, and that war is the father of all things …. In the self-identity of completely diverging, oppositional things, in disharmonious harmony: *there* is life, and the appearance of this disharmonious harmony, of this contradictory self-identity, is the species. In the mutual opposition and conflict of individual versus individual, the formation of the species takes place" (Nishida 1978 – 80c, 100-1).

I said earlier that Leibniz's "metaphysical mechanism" seems to give the Leibnizian universe a certain Darwinian spin, and, arguably, something similar can be said about Nishida's "historical world." Alternatively, one might think of Adam Smith's "invisible hand," which inspired Darwin's theory. In any case, Nishida's "world" is a "Heraclitean world," as he himself repeatedly emphasizes, and, as I would like to add, a pretty Hegelian one as well: "a *Volk* … as a particular, individual entity … is exclusive of other, similar individuals," and for this reason, "the conflict between them becomes a relationship of violence, a state of war," as Hegel asserts in his argument against Kant's idea of a "league of princes" for achieving a state of "eternal peace" (1986, 345-346). Of course, Heraclitus' "war" is just a metaphor, and Nishida's "struggle" too does not necessarily have to be interpreted as physical war. Yet, it certainly does not imply any Kantian League of Nations either (cf. the preamble of the League) or any order based on what Nishida's disciple Nishitani Keiji occasionally called the "dubious ideal" of a unity of individuals respecting each other in their freedom and equality: "the recognition of the freedom of the other … has in mind only the empty, abstract 'human being', respectively the empty abstract 'nation' …. Accordingly, any such order of freedom and equality must remain merely formal" (Chūō kōron 1943, 84). Such a merely formal, artificial order, as Nishida points out in his "Principle," has no effect on reality. His own "new world order," by contrast, is supposed to be one that emerges spontaneously and organically out of the natural "struggle" and the free, unhampered interplay of the internal "powers" and inner potentials of the "living species"; this order, as I would like to conclude, is quite a romantic and utterly reactionary political vision. This, however, probably also explains the popularity, which Nishida enjoys today, especially in certain neo-romantic academic circles, which, in the shadow of the neo-liberal morphing of global capitalism, are likewise obsessed with "cultural difference" and "identity." Thus, reactionary times feature reactionary ideologies.

REFERENCES

Adorno, Theodor Wiesengrund 1997. *Negative Dialektik* (Negative Dialectics). Frankfurt am Main: Suhrkamp.

Aristotle 1991, *Metaphysik. Zweiter Halbband, Bücher VII (Z)–XIV (N) Griechisch– Deutsch* (Metaphysics. Second Volume, Books VII (Z)–XIV (N) Greek-German). Revised translation by Herman Bonitz, introduced, commented on, and edited by Horst Seidel. Hamburg: Meiner Verlag.

Chūō kōron sha 1943. Sōryokusen no tetsugaku. Zadankai (The Philosophy of Total War. Symposium). In: *Chūō kōron,* Jan. 1943, 54–112.

Hegel, Georg Wilhelm Friedrich 1969. *Wissenschaft der Logik II* (Greater Logic, volume II), *Theorie-Werkausgabe G. W. F. Hegel, Werke in zwanzig Bänden, 6* (Theory-Work-Edition G. W. F. Hegel, Works in Twenty Volumes, vol. 6). Frankfurt am Main: Suhrkamp Verlag.

Hegel, Georg Wilhelm Friedrich 1986. *Enzyklopädie der Philosophischen Wissenschaften im Grundrisse. Dritter Teil. Die Philosophie des Geistes. Mit den mündlichen Zusätzen* (Outline of the Encyclopedia of the Philosophical Sciences. The Philosophy of the Spirit. Third Part. With the Oral Additions). *Werke in zwanzig Bänden, 10* (Works in 20 Volumes, vol. 10). Frankfurt am Main: Suhrkamp Verlag.

Kant, Immanuel 1968. *Kritik der reinen Vernunft 1* (Critique of Pure Reason, vol. 1), *Theorie-Werkausgabe Immanuel Kant, Werke in 12 Bänden* (Theory-Work-Edition Immanuel Kant, Works in Twelve Volumes), vol. III. Edited by Wilhelm Weischedel. Frankfurt am Main: Suhrkamp Verlag.

Karatani Kōjin 1994. *'Senzen' no shikō* (Thinking of the "Pre-War"). Tokyo: Bungei bungakusha.

Leibniz, Gottfried Wilhelm 1960: *Fragmente zur Logik* (Fragments Concerning Logic). Selected, translated and annotated by Franz Schmidt. Berlin: Akademie-Verlag.

Leibniz, Gottfried Wilhelm 1966: *Fünf Schriften zur Logik und Metaphysik* (Five Writings on Logic and Metaphysics). Translated by Herbert Herring. Stuttgart: Reclam Verlag.

Leibniz, Gottfried Wilhelm 1982a: Monadologie (Monadology). In *Vernunftprinzipien der Natur und der Gnade. Monadologie. Französisch–deutsch* (Principles of Nature and Grace, Based on Reason. Monadology. French–German), 26–69. On the basis of the critical edition by André Robinet (1954) and the translation by Arthur Buchenau. Edited and annotated by Herbert Herring. Hamburg, Meiner Verlag.

Leibniz, Gottfried Wilhelm 1982b: Vernunftprinzipien der Natur und der Gnade (Principles of Nature and Grace, Grounded in Reason). In *Vernunftprinzipien der Natur und der Gnade. Monadologie. Französisch–deutsch* (Principles of Nature and Grace, Based on Reason. Monadology. French–German), 2–25. On the basis of the critical edition by André Robinet (1954) and the translation by Arthur Buchenau. Edited and annotated by Herbert Herring. Hamburg, Meiner Verlag.

Leibniz, Gottfried Wilhelm 1991: *Metaphysische Abhandlung* (Discourse on Metaphysics). Translated and annotated by Herbert Herring. Reprint of the revised edition of 1985. Hamburg: Meiner Verlag.

Leibniz, Gottfried Wilhelm 1999a. La Vraie Methode (The True Method). In *Sämtliche Schriften und Briefe* (Complete Works and Letters; hereafter: SSB), *Reihe VI: Philosophische Schriften, Band 4: 1677-1690* (Series VI: Philosophical Writings, Volume 4: 1677–1690), 3–7. Berlin: Akademie-Verlag.

Leibniz, Gottfried Wilhelm 2000. *Die Grundlagen des Logischen Kalküls. Fundamenta calculi logici. Lateinisch-deutsch* (The Foundations of the Logical Calculus. *Fundamenta calculi logici*. Latin-German). Edited, translated, introduced and annotated by Franz Schupp and Stephanie Weber. Hamburg: Meiner Verlag.

Nishida Kitarō 1978-80a. Sekai shin chitsujo no genri (The Principle of the New World Order). In *Nishida Kitarō Zenshū* (Complete Works of Nishida Kitarō; herafter: *NKZ*), Vol. 12, 427-434. Tokyo: Iwanami shoten.

Nishida Kitarō 1978-80b. Sekai no jiko dōitsu to renzoku (Self-Identity and Continuity of the World). In *NKZ*, vol. 8, 7-106. Tokyo: Iwanami shoten.

Nishida Kitarō 1978-80c. Rekishiteki sekai ni oite no kobutsu no tachiba (The Standpoint of the Individual in the Historical World)). In *NKZ*, vol. 9, 69-146. Tokyo: Iwanami shoten.

Nishida Kitarō 1978-80d. Kōiteki chokkan no tachiba (The Standpoint of Active Intuition). In *NKZ*, vol. 8, 107-218. Tokyo: Iwanami shoten.

Nishida Kitarō 1978-80e. Ronri to seimei (Logic and Life). In *NKZ*, vol. 8, 273-394. Tokyo: Iwanami shoten.

Nishida Kitarō 1978-80f. Zushikiteki setsumei 1 [Graphical Explanation, no. 1]. In *NKZ*, vol. 8, 219-266. Tokyo: Iwanami shoten.

Nishida Kitarō 1978-80g. Basho (Place). In *NKZ*, vol. 4, 207-289. Tokyo: Iwanami shoten.

Nishida Kitarō 1978-80h. Keijijōgakuteki tachiba kara mita Tōsei kodai no bunka keitai (The Forms of the Antique Cultures in the east amd the West, Seen from a Metaphysical Point of View). In *NKZ*, vol. 7, 429-453. Tokyo: Iwanami shoten.

Nishida Kitarō 1978-80i. Chishiki no kyakkansei ni tsuite aratanaru chishikiron no chiban" (On the Objectivity of Knowledge. A Foundation for a New Theory of Knowledge). In *NKZ*, vol. 10, 343-476. Tokyo: Iwanami shoten.

Nishida Kitarō 1978-80j. Shu no seisei hatten no mondai (The Problem of the Emergence and Development of the Species), *NKZ*, vol. 8, 500-540. Tokyo: Iwanami shoten.

Nishida Kitarō 1978-80k. Nihon bunka no mondai (The Question of Japanese Culture), *NKZ* , vol. 12. 279-383. Tokyo: Iwanami shoten.

Nishida Kitarō 1987. *Last Writings: Nothingness and the Religious World View*. Translated by David Dilworth. Honolulu: University of Hawaii Press.

Schupp, Franz 2003: *Geschichte der Philosophie im Überblick* (Review of the History of Philosophy), *Band 3: Neuzeit* (Volume 3: The Modern Era). Hamburg: Meiner Verlag.

[Symposium]
Alternatives to Hegemonic International Relations:
The Kyoto-school Categories

Chih-yu SHIH
Department of Political Science
National Taiwan University

In the mainstream literature of international relations (IR), the nature of world politics is essentially war and peace premised on state-centrism and undergirded by one superpower and other major powers, which is primarily exemplified by the US and by western European countries. Hegemonic IR contradict with and transform non-western world orders elsewhere, including the East Asian cases of Japan, Taiwan, and China, resulting in their ambivalence toward their pasts. The philosophy of place (PoP) advocated by the Kyoto School provides clarity on the identity puzzle of Japan and of other nations with a similar problem by asking the possibility of a nation to represent both East and West, leading to a non-western, non-territorial, or non-centrist position. The puzzle emphasizes the aim of Japan for normalcy of in-betweenness (Shimizu 2014, Josuke 2008), which is a statement of alienation from hegemonic IR. In the subsequent discussion, the theory of "hegemonic IR" refers to the nature of world politics being dominated by a single discourse.

Western modernity demonstrates a strong need to convert others from a differing trajectory to a common, that is, universal, destiny. In contrast to hegemonic IR, the Kyoto School of Philosophy (KSP) conceives the idea of universalism as one of becoming others. Universalism is enhanced by accommodating or acquiring additional thoughts and identities in one's own self-imagination. As a bridge between civilizations, conversion and synthesis are redundant, if not harmful (Shimizu 2009). Instead for KSP, a strong need for self-conversion exists so that the adoption of Western modernity can enhance the degree of Japan's universalism. Under such self-concept, Japan remains to be the sole nation that is capable of constantly becoming others to eventually encompass all. In fact, the Pacific War that the Japanese military launched against the US proceeded exactly in the name of the universalist "World History Standpoint (WHS)", with the aim of exposing the partial nature of Western modernity. The mission provided by WHS was allegedly "to overcome modernity". This mission was not to deny modernity in its entirety, but to transcend the partial nature of western modernity. The other side of the coin was to modernize the rest of "the Greater East Asia", which the Japanese military considered as the entirety of the Japanese self.

The double missions were therefore to defeat the partial West and to convert the backward portion of the East Asian self. Nishida wished that differing nations can meet without mutual naming or judgment. Accordingly, Japan's in-between place is presumably a place of nothingness or a non-place, where Idealistically Japan exemplifies a civilizational origin and bridge that enables the East to meet the West and vice versa. The assumption of PoP is that neither the East nor the West should expand or conquer the other. Their commonality must not lie in the teleological historiography because preservation of their difference is the spirit that guarantees their inclusion in a universal world, resulting in the multi-directionality of WHS. Where the multi-directionality of WHS is present, the coexistence of East and West can only be traced to a shared origin where all come from and each flourishes on its own condition. The origin that lies deeper than the consciousness of difference is by definition the place of nothingness. PoP is therefore not the same concept of self-other as that mentioned in the literature on identity (Connlly 2002). The formulation of PoP is thus easily connected with the imagined origin of the universe and is practically coupled with Japanese Shinto, which provides a metaphor of the origin of Japan. For PoP, both the self and its others are non-synthesized identities to be gathered by an ultimate being in nothingness.

From the past dynastic China to Communist China and then to the rise of capitalist China, the Chinese people have practically accepted the co-existence of Western values, identities, and institutions in their political life. However, China has suffered (or perhaps enjoyed) false, insincere, and incompatible learning. The difficulty that Japan had encountered with the backward East Asia, particularly China, was its incapacity for effective learning. For the Japanese, this disadvantage suggests China's incapacity for true learning. According to the classic Japanese explanation (Tanaka

1993), which remains popular after the ongoing reform in China, China's over-reliance on rituals to harmonize relationships with superior invaders has hindered the country from achieving authentic modernity. In this formulation, China appears to have the capability to accommodate differing values and identities by ritually relating them. However, China does not learn at a level deeper than the instrumental use of alien civilization. Therefore, the Chinese claim to universality is nominal, spurious, and lacks appreciation, despite the similar capability to facilitate coexistence of Western modernity and Chinese culture. In the KHS perspective, China by itself is unable to resist the West, nor engage in serious reform. As a result, learning is at best partial and eventually reduced to harmonizing and stabilizing a relationship.

Japan should exemplify for the West and East Asia the process of entering and withdrawing from the site of their existential experiences to exercise re-entry. To become more genuinely universal, Japan executes both entry into and withdrawal from any partial identities that are not to be synthesized. One has to consider "place" as a metaphor of identity, along with the notion of site. For Japan, in contrast to Western modernity, the exercise of withdrawing from a specific "place" to "no place" allows the imagination of freedom from either one's own past or Western modernity. This withdrawal, called self-denial, also allows further imagination of re-entry from nothingness into many potentially differing sites, including that of the intruder. The metaphor of nothingness exclusively provides Japan with the capability to see the limitation of all sites, including the alleged hegemony and all strings of universalism, and then the celebration of an emerging world history that accommodates and transcends all sites is achieved.

KHS demonstrates cultivates an archetypal subjectivity to transcend any mundane conditions. Framing Western modernity, East Asian resistance, and Chinese management of relationship, along with Japan's WHS, PoP categorizes "place" into four different types (Ng, 2011; Huang W. H. 2010). First, a place of being/identity is an absolute place trapped in false rationalism and universalism, such as Western modernity. This place constitutes contemporary hegemonism. Second, a place of relative being/identity is a relative place that resists hegemonism, such as the quest of East Asia for indigenous identity in Taiwan, Korea, Vietnam, and so on, in which re-worlding belongs. A typical formulation of relative being is postcolonial hybridity. Imagined nationalities, as well as aboriginality, are stronger versions of a relative identity. Third, a place of relative nothingness is a transcendental place to connect or permeate places as well as relative places, such as the Chinese scheme of relating to each other in specific contexts, which include balance of relationship (BoR). One example is Chinese Daoism, while another can be non-alignment by Jawaharlal Nehru. Finally, a place of absolute nothingness is where time and space meet to render the other three places thinkable and seeable.

The abovementioned second place is the place of relative identity uses the emerging, contemporary IR expression of "worldliness". Creating worldliness of a site is essentially worlding it. In the past, worlding was a geo-cultural project of global capitalism/hegemony to monopolize meanings (Petman, 1996; Spivak, 1985). Resisting this project is known as re-worlding, a form of self-worlding that emerges from a supposedly subaltern site for and by the self. Re-worlding is a discursive reclaim of the lost soul by excavating, retrieving, reviving, and rejuvenating a narrative of the past. Sited worlding results in a declaration that hegemonic power cannot monopolize either ontological or epistemological resources. Sited worlding resists, undermines, or revises a hegemonic division of work through uncontrollable fluidity caused by the incongruent schemata of the subalterns, their ideological inconsistency, opportunism, self-denial, and self-assertion (Paolini, Elliott, and Moran, 1996). Sited worlding critically assesses any hegemonic attempt to reproduce dominance over subalterns.

Victimized people reincarnate by looking back through an imagined subjectivity belonging exclusively to the site, which is not subject to universalism. That's why the methods of re-worlding must be multiplied and improvised as both recast memories of various forms, and their re-interpretations serve as methods to reach testimonies to differences, aimed at thinking back on hegemonic arrangements of lives at the subaltern sites as well as writing and acting back to provincialize hegemonic order. In other words, worlding incurs the site-centric methodology and aims at cultivating a counter perspective in the face of an overwhelming hegemony. The editors of the *Routledge Worlding Beyond the West Series* declare that "[t]he aim of worlding is to explore the role of geocultural factors in setting the concepts and epistemologies through which IR knowledge is produced. In particular, worlding seeks to identify alternatives for thinking about the "international" that are more in tune with local concerns and traditions outside the West (Tickner and Waever, 2009, Blurb)."

The aforementioned third place is the place of relative nothingness. It also has a parallel in the nascent IR literature, that is, in the Chinese School. A number of Chinese schools invest in Chinese cultural resources that formulate general theories of IR; hence, Daoism, Confucianism, and Legalism are employed to examine the coexistence of differences (Zhao 2009), relational reciprocity (Qin 2009), and benevolent hierarchy (Yan 2011). Together, they indicate a shared longing for an order that can transcend the self-interests of individual nations. As a result, the quest for a relational order subscribes to no specific institution or value. An example can be found in the arrangement between the Chinese dynastic court and its neighbors or between the late Qing court and various imperial powers, which was flexibly designed to meet the differing conditions of each tributary state or imperialist power, upon which the two sides build their relationship (Liao, 2012). Aside from the distinctiveness of each bilateral relationship, the rules that have governed China over the generations are hardly ever the same; thus, the Chinese considers an imagined cycle of governability and chaos as typical and still officially sanctioned at present (see, for example, Jiang, 2012). If the spontaneity of cycles discontinues because of rationalist intervention, governability will lose its trajectory and may never resume, leaving brutal force as the only viable solution to anarchy.

BoR pragmatically adopts a laissez-faire approach in handling the domestic chaos of a partner. According to the aforementioned Japanese criticism of Chinese over-reliance on ritual and relationship, the Chinese intellectual history is not particularly keen to the adoption of Western institutions or values. Chinese international relationship is therefore highly independent from value or institution consideration. Chinese international relationship is likewise not particularly strong in ensuring defense against invaders. Both local gentries and the dynastic courts look for ways to coexist with invading powers. Achieving a balanced relationship is the quintessential philosophy of life that seeks to transcend the power difference by establishing reciprocal relationships. To maintain a balanced relationship, China should yield to the other side as long as the challenge to the existing relationship is not judged as malicious. By yielding, China's exhibits sincerity toward the relationship. In addition, China must resist vehemently if the violation is anticipated to be detrimental to a long-term relationship, despite China's relative weakness in power. This resistance shows China's determination to restore the correct relationship (Huang and Shih 2014). These two principles of a balanced relationship, namely, yielding and resistance to the perceived degree of challenge to a relationship, are essentially subversive to hegemonic IR that is founded on power, interest, and value, although both principles are inconsequential from the KHS perspective. When both domestic cycles and balance of power are disconnected from Chinese international relations, any multilateral arrangement to channel intervention or synchronic value to justify the disconnection would be redundant.

If IR can be reduced to a combination of bilateral relations, other universal learning is no longer necessary as the source of good governance at present may become the source of chaos in the next cycle and vice versa. Anything that fades at the present can return to consciousness given the right cue. Ultimately, only reciprocal relationships are practical and transcendent (Hwang Kwang Kuo, 2012), and if China cultivates positive long-term relationships, others will always reciprocate depending on capability. Values and ideologies become irrelevant once the relationship is stabilized, and domestic problems are subsequently not the duty of others to resolve. When given sufficient time, solutions can be obtained domestically. Patience, instead of forced transformation, is the main characteristic in BoR in Chinese international relations theory and is known as the "Great Way" in Chinese discourse, upon which all strangers supposedly walk together harmoniously alongside the self-cultivating prince (Ames and Hall, 2003). After all, what would be the excitement in forcing a conversion in a subaltern site when one knows that nothing will remain the same in the long run?

Lastly, the foundational place, according to a KSP scholar, is the place of absolute nothingness. It is exempted from all cultural maneuverings that maintain relational stability and, under the condition of nothingness, transcendence replaces resistance (Nishitani, 1983). The place of absolute nothingness is composed of pure experience, according to Nishida, prior to the acquisition of any meaning. In all of the encounters with differing societies in the past, as well as those in the future, the vicissitudes experienced in one's own society and the transcendent attempts to move beyond sited limitations occur in the place of absolute nothingness.

The place of absolute nothingness provides both peaceful and violent unpredictable clues and calms all conflicts, with or without justice. The place of absolute nothingness contains the sources of cycles, prompts new cycles, or reversely represses them. Hegemonies are possible but never permanent or universal. Multi-sited worlding and re-worlding never stop, but they guarantee no single result or success.

The lack of duty is even greater than in the place of relative nothingness because, while relative nothingness cultivates a small sense of duty toward any pretentiously universal cause, one can lose the sense of duty toward his/her life and that of others in insensible and insensitive nothingness (Heisig and Maraldo, 1995; Hubbard and Swanson, 1997). Practically, the freedom to act and the quest for the freedom to act beyond the physical limit testify the fearless spirit being expected of Japan that owns WHS. This fearlessness includes in self-becoming and self-disciplining on one hand and in overcoming the physical restraint imposed by the materialistic civilization of the West on the other hand. The constant self-becoming indicates the spirit of continuous self-denial required of Japan and East Asia to exercise withdrawal from one's own limited place of relative identity. The place of absolute nothingness is most properly represented by the arrival of an international society centering on the principle of in-betweenness.

To achieve this kind of international society, self-denial is the essential characteristic to show because Japan has to display to the rest of the world its transcendent capacity for being anyone else. Without extensive self-denial from its East-Asian qualities, Japan would not be able to become as good as or better than other civilizations by the standard of the latter. Thus, Japan would not be free or universal. Each entry is highly extreme that Japan endeavors to become more modern than the West or to become more practiced in Sinology than China. Learning leads to the unlikely withdrawal to nothingness for those already involved in faithful learning until they are physically or socially exhausted at further perfection. In fact, pre-WWII Japan considered itself as the best pupil of Sinology and as the genuine successor of the Chinese culture to sustain and improve its modern fate (Tanaka 1993). Given the country's Sinological spirit, Japan's acquisition of modernity proceeded at a level much higher than the materialistic civilization of the West, which provides the identity of in-betweenness that fully describes the international society. This quality is unavailable in the place of relative nothingness where learning is insincere and relational coupling is more important than learning.

In total, there are four places of PoP — place of absolute identity, place of relative identity, place of relative nothingness, and place of absolute nothingness. The construction of PoP begins with absolute indentity's synchronizing project. In Table I, this is in the left bottom. Synchronization should be considered as an enactment of place of absolute identity, while synchronicity is the derivative of rationalism and universalism and informs most general theories in IR. Synchronization refers to the simultaneous execution or promoted diffusion of a pattern of rational thinking embedded in an idea, an institution, a collective identity, or a perceived arrangement of material force. Synchronization is presumably a process in which unrelated national actors conjunctionally fulfill their self-assigned functions to interact rationally. Accordingly, synchronization is the exact opposite of absolute nothingness.

Table I: The PoP Conditions of Identity

Multi-sited	Synchronic	Yes	No
Yes		Philosophy of Place as Absolute nothingness	Worlding as Relative identity
No		Hegemonic Order as Absolute identity	Balance of Relationships as Relative nothingness

Source: The author

Ames, Roger and David Hall. 2003. *Laozi, Dao De Jing: A Philosophical Translation*. New York: Ballantine Books.
Connolly, William. 2002. *Identity\Difference: Democratic Negotiations of Political Paradox*. Minneapolis: University of Minnesota Press.
Huang, Chia-ning and Shih, Chih-yu. 2009. *No Longer Oriental: Self and European Characteristics in Japan's Views on China*. Taipei: The Research and Educational Center for China Studies and Cross Taiwan-Strait Relations, Department of Political Science, National Taiwan University.
Huang, Wen-hong. 2010. "Xitian jiduolang changsuo luoji de neizai zhuanxiang" (The Internal Turn in Nishida Kitaro's Logic of Place). *National Chengchi University Journal 23: 1-31*.
Hubbard, James and Paul Swanson. Eds. 1997. *Pruning the Bodhi Tree: The Storm Over Critical Buddhism*. Honolulu: University of Hawaii Press.
Hwang, Kwang-kuo. 2012. *Foundations of Chinese Psychology: Confucian Social Relations*. New York: Springer.
Jiang, Zeming. 2012. "Gaodu zhongshi zhonghua minzu fazhan shi" (Highly Stress Chinese

National History of Development). In Chinese Academy of Social Science. Ed. *Easy Readers for Chinese History* (jianming zhongguo lishi duben). Beijing: Chinese Social Science Press. Preface.

Josuke, Ikeda. 2008. "Japanese Vision of International Society: A Historical Exploration." In Kosuke Shimizu, Josuke Ikeda, Tomoya Kamino and Shiro Sato, Eds. *Is There A Japanese IR? Seeking an Academic Bridge through Japan's History of International Relations*. Ryukoku: Afrasian Centre for Peace and Development Studies, Ryukoku University.

Liao, Minshu. 2012. "Diplomatic Order of Qing China" (Qingdai zhongguo de waizheng zhisu). In Editor n.a. Ed. *Jindai zhongguo: wenhua yu waijiao* (*Modern China: Culture and Diplomacy*). Beijing: Social Science Literature Press, pp. 130-153.

Nishitani, Keiji. 1983. *Religion and Nothingness*. Berkeley: University of California Press.

Ng, Yu-kwan. 2011. "Juedui wu yu zhexue guannian de dianfan" (Absolute Nothingness and the Paradigms of Philosophical Concepts). *Zhengguan* 56: 5-28.

Paolini, Albert J., Anthony Elliott, and Anthony Moran. 1999. *Navigating Modernity: Postcolonialism, Identity, and International Relations*. Boulder, US: Lynne Rienner.

Pettman, Jan Jindy. 1996. *Worlding Women: A Feminist International Politics*. London: Routledge.

Qin, Yaqing. 2009. "Guanxi Benwei yu Guocheng Jiangou: Jiang Zhongguo Linian Zhiru Guoji Guuanxi Lilun" (Relationality and Processual Construction: Bring Chinese Ideas into IRT). *Social Sciences in China*, No. 3: 69–86.

Shimizu, Kosuke. 2014. "Materializing the 'non-Western': two stories of Japanese philosophers on culture and politics in the inter-war period." *Cambridge Review of International Affairs*. DOI: 10.1080/09557571.2014.889083

Shimizu, Kosuke. 2009. "Nishida Kitaro and Japan's Interwar Foreign Policy: War Involvement and Culturalist Political Discourse." *Working Paper Series* 44. Kyoto: Arasian Centre for Peace and Development Studies.

Spivak, Gayatri Chakravorty. 1985. "Three Women's Texts and A Critique of Imperialism." *Critique Inquiry* 12, 1: 235-161.

Tickner, Arlene and Ole Waever. 2009. International Relations Scholarship Around the World. London: Routledge.

Tanaka, Stephen. 1993. *Japan's Orient: Rendering the Past into the Future*. Berkeley: University of California Press.

Yan, Xuetong. 2011. *Ancient Chinese Thought and Modern Chinese Power*, ed. Daniel Bell and Zhe Sun, trans. Edmund Ryden. Princeton: Princeton University Press.

Zhao, Tingyang. 2009. "A Political World Philosophy in Terms of All-under-heaven (Tian-xia)." *Diogenes* 221: 5-18.

[Symposium]
Tekhnē, Culture and the New Order:
The Elimination of Politics by Nishida Kitarō

Satofumi KAWAMURA
Project Assistant Professor
The University of Tokyo Center for Philosophy

Introduction

Nishida Kitarō (1870-1945) is one of the most contentious philosophers because of his involvement with war-time politics. He published politico-philosophical works, such as *The Problem of Japanese Culture* (*Nihon bunka no mondai*) (Nishida 2004b) and "The Principle of the World New Order" (*Sekai shin-chitsujo no genri*), which could be interpreted as glorifications of the Emperor-centred Japanese culture (or Japanese spirit) and the ideology of the Greater East-Asia Co-prosperity Sphere (*Dai-tōa kyōei-ken*). Furthermore, his disciples, the so-called thinkers of the "Kyoto School" (*Kyoto gakuha*), actively addressed the necessity to overcome the "imperialistic" Western modernity through the war waged by Japan. In particular, they participated in the symposium sponsored by *Chuo koron*, which played a crucial role in spreading the dictum of "Overcoming Modernity" (*Kindai no chōkoku*). For example, Nishitani Keiji, a senior member of the Kyoto School, argued that the Western imperialistic subjectivity could be overcome only by the subjectivity based on the traditional Oriental philosophy of "nothingness" (*Mu-teki shutai*), and this was precisely the purpose of the Greater East Asia Co-prosperity Sphere (*Dai-tōa kyōeiken*) (Nishitani 1979). The notion of "nothingness" (*Mu*) was clearly conceived under the strong influence of Nishida's philosophy. As a scholar of Chinese literature, Takeuchi Yoshimi, argues (Takeuchi 1979, 274) that "Overcoming Modernity" was a buzzword that strongly appealed to intellectuals because, as the critic Yamada Munemutsu points out (Yamada 1975, 65–67), the discourse of "Overcoming Modernity" provided many students with a compelling excuse to resolve their internal struggle with the question, "Why should I go to the battlefield?" by legitimating the war waged by the Japanese as being for the emancipation of Asian countries from the modern Western imperialist powers.

Nishida has been denounced as an accomplice of the wartime ideologues, such as ultra-nationalists (*chō-kokka-shugi sha*), militarists, or Asianists (*Ajia-shugi sha*). By the same token, there have also been many attempts by the followers of Nishida and members of the Kyoto School to refute such denouncements. His followers argue that Nishida's intention was not to justify ultra-nationalist and militarist ideology, but rather to try to dissent from them. According to them, although Nishida shared the same ideological terms, such as *Shin-chitsujo* (New Order), *Hakkōichiu* (the Eight Corners of the World under One Roof) or *Kōdō* (Imperial way), with ultra-nationalists or militarists, the reason why Nishida used these terms was that he tried to modify the direction in which Japan was forced to go by them, re-interpreting dominant political concepts from his philosophical standpoint. This is the so-called semantic "Tug of War" (*Imi no sōdatsu-sen*), referred to by Ueda Shizuteru (Ueda 1995). From this point of view, Nishida's involvement with wartime politics should be understood as a dissent from the social and political trends at the time.

In this paper, I shall examine Nishida's political discourse in terms of "politics" because, in my opinion, his political discourse strives to eliminate "politics" and this contributed to the reinforcement of the existing order. Considering Nishida's personal sentiment, I shall argue that he has a strong aversion to wartime policies and that his initiatives were usurped by militarists and ultra-nationalists. It is easy to verify this fact by browsing through his diaries, written during the 1930s and 40s. In fact, Nishida tried to construct a logic which did not legitimate any violence or atrocities enacted on Asian people by Japan in the name of great causes like the World New Order. However, his attempt worked to hide or repress the conflict or dispute which was necessarily caused by political settings. In other words, Nishida's logic eliminated any possibility of politics, in Jacques Rancière's sense, which would necessary occur in the moment to build a political order. This is what I have referred to as the elimination of politics and, because of this elimination, Nishida's political discourse cannot be seen to be critical of the existing political order or to posit a reality beyond the existing order.

1. Poiesis and Praxis

In order to elucidate how Nishida eliminated politics, I shall first of all look at his discussion on the state. According to Nishida, the state must be underpinned by a rational principle which he refers to as the "reason of state" (*Kokka-riyū*). This is the translation of *raison d'état* or *Staatsräson*. Nishida borrowed this notion from Mainecke's *The Idea of Reason of State* (*Die Idee Der Staatsräson*). As Nishida translates reason as "*riyū*", he believes that the state should have a rational reason for existence – "why the state should exist". In other words, for Nishida, a state which has such a rational reason can legitimate its existence. However, the question is, what is the rational reason for the existence of the state?

This is the central question Nishida raises in his essay titled "The Problem of Reason of State" (*Kokka-riyū no mondai*), published in 1941, three months before the start of the Asia-Pacific War. This question leads Nishida to contemplate the problem of the relationship between subject and *tekhnē* and he examines the problematique of *praxis* and *poiesis* in order to elucidate the relationship. As a result, Nishida reaches the conclusion that subject is the subject of *praxis* (practice) and that the subject practices *poiesis* (making or producing) in his/her *praxis*, believing that *tekhnē* is necessary to ensure this *praxis* and *poiesis*.

Prior to the publication of *The Problem of Reason of State*, Nishida discussed the problematique of *praxis* and *poiesis* in the essay titled "Poiesis and Praxis" (*Poieshisu to purakushisu*) (Nishida 2004a) in 1940. In this essay, Nishida argues that *praxis* and *poiesis* have a seemingly contradictory relationship, because while *praxis* is based on a transcendent principle, *poiesis* is based on an immanent principle. Nishida defines *praxis* as the practice of doing something according to rationality or reason. As reason is the faculty that facilitates the positing of a generalising principle, which transcends and codifies concrete experiences, for Nishida, *praxis* is the practice of creating, codifying or ordering according to such a transcendent and generalising principle. By contrast, Nishida is convinced that *poiesis* has to be immanent to concrete experiences, because to make or produce something means to understand what has to be made. For example, if you want to make a good house, you have to know what kind of house you need at the time. Furthermore, the house you need will determine what kind of materials you have to use to build it. Therefore, *poiesis*, as the practice of making or creating something, is to understand the concrete condition or context in which you are embedded and going to take action.

Although Nishida understands that *praxis* contradicts *poiesis*, he thinks that in the process of *praxis* the subject necessarily has to pursue *poiesis*. This is because Nishida is convinced that *praxis* is the practice through which the subject realises his/her true individual character (*shin no kosei*). According to him, the individual defines his/her subjectivity by ordering or codifying the world and through the formation of his/her subjectivity the individual expresses his/her true individual character. As the practice of creating, ordering or codification has to follow the reason or generalising principle, Nishida claims that the individual subjectivity has to be formed or defined according to the generalising principle and that the true individual character is also expressed by following the generalising principle. This process is the essence of *praxis*. Therefore, Nishida defines *praxis* as the practice of realising the true individual character according to the generalising principle. However, Nishida also argues that the true individual character can be expressed through concrete experiences. In particular, the experience of making something is more likely to express the individual character of the subject who made it. In this sense, the true individual character of the subject is more likely to be expressed through *poiesis*. This true individual character, expressed through *poiesis*, is likely to deviate from the generalising principle because *poiesis*, based on concrete experiences, will produce diversity or plurality, which cannot completely be defined by the generalising principle.

Thus, despite their apparent contradictory relationship, *praxis* necessarily involves *poiesis*. Nishida believes that this contradiction is the moment at which a totality emerges: a totality which could subsume each true individual character. According to Nishida, this totality is embodied as the state. Nishida claims that the state establishes the general order according to which people interpret the world: that is, the state provides the generalising principle for *praxis*. At the same time, Nishida argues that the state consists of the concrete life of each individual: that is, within the state, people create something new in their concrete lives and thereby express their true individual characters in diverse ways as their particular or unique *poiesis*. Nishida is convinced that the state can reflect the diversity or plurality produced through each person's *poiesis* in the general order, because the totality embodied by the state is constituted by this diversity or plurality.

In short, the state emerges as the mediation or dialectic of the contradiction between *praxis* and *poiesis*: the state mediates the transcendent generalising principle and the immanent diversity or plurality and therefore becomes both the concrete realm, where the true individual character of each subject is expressed and the generalising principle which defines the true character of each subject. In other words, in the state, the individual becomes the subject of *praxis* and *poiesis*: the subject who codifies the world according to the order provided by the state and creates something new, which becomes a constitutive element of the totality embodied by the state. Of course, he does not argue that any state can mediate the contradiction. For him, there is a particular state which can mediate the contradiction and only this type of state upholds "reason of state". However, how is it possible to envisage a state that upholds "reason of state"? To answer this question, we have to focus on Nishida's concept of *tekhnē* and culture.

2. *Tekhnē* and Culture: Elimination of Politics under the Name of Culture

One may well ask whether it is possible to construct a state that is underpinned by "reason of state". In order to consider this question, Nishida discusses the concepts of *tekhnē* (*gijutsu*) and culture. According to Nishida, a state, underpinned by "reason of state", has to be grounded on culture, because culture is precisely the totality which can mediate the contradiction between *praxis* and *poiesis*. In other words, the state is an institutional system based on a culture and *tekhnē* is necessary to establish such an institutional system. Nishida is convinced that the aim of politics is to establish a state underpinned by "reason of state" and, in order to achieve this aim, politics needs *tekhnē* as the art or technology to establish an institutional system which reflects culture.

In *The Problem of Japanese Culture*, which was published as a book in the Iwanami Shinsho series in 1940, Nishida states:

> In human society, according to [the dialectic of] the contradictory self-identity of the one as totality and the many as individuals, each

individual sustains him/herself; [in human society] the prosperity of the species leads to the prosperity of [each] individual, and vice versa… Thus, the formation of human beings [in species as ethnic society] is something called [the formation of] culture; [the formation of culture is] the formation of species [as ethnic society] and of [the individual who has the sense of] the self in species; species [as ethnic society] is the world [developing] according to [the dialectic of] the absolute contradictory self-identity [between human beings]. Hence the formation of human beings is the self-formation of the historical world, and it must mean the creation [of the historical world] (Nishida 2004b, 45).

According to Nishida, the dialectic between *praxis* and *poiesis* forms culture as a species (*shu*). Culture is the totality which mediates the contradiction between *praxis* and *poiesis*, and therefore the totality has "the contradictory self-identity of the one as totality and the many as individuals [who are the subjects of *poiesis*]". Nishida is also convinced that the formation of culture is the formation of species and that such a cultural species is realised as an ethnic nation (*minzoku*). Thus, as an ethnic or national culture, as the totality is formed, the individual becomes the subject, both to codify the world and to reproduce the world through creating something new in the world. The reproduction of the world makes history and Nishida therefore emphasises the formation of "the historical world" (*rekishi-teki sekai*) through the formation of culture.

As culture is the ethnic or national culture, a state based on such an ethnic or national culture, is the nation-state. Therefore, *tekhnē* is the art or technology to establish a nation-state as an institutional system underpinned by "reason of state". However, what is *tekhnē* in concrete terms? For Nishida, it is law (*hō*), or more precisely, the institutional system underpinned by law. Nishida argues that, to establish the nation-state, means to establish the legal institutional system (*hō-sei*). In other words, the nation-state is established as the institutional system and the framework of the institutional system is underpinned by law. While law is the code according to which people understand the world, law has to reflect or be subject to people's concrete experiences through which they create something new. In this sense, law is the appropriate *tekhnē* to establish the nation-state, which mediates the contradiction.

Nishida also discusses the problem of the legislator (*rippō-sha*), but it does not matter for him who the actual legislator in the institution is. For him, if the mediation or dialectic between *praxis* and *poiesis* operates correctly, it is not necessary to ask who has the real power to decide on the law. Therefore, Nishida discusses only sovereignty and actually never mentions the sovereign (*shukensha*). By avoiding attributing sovereignty to a concrete person, he posits sovereignty as the prerogative of the state itself, because the state, as the embodiment of the mediation between *praxis* and *poiesis*, has the legitimacy to exercise the prerogative. In this sense, the legislator is merely an agency of the state.

According to Nishida, the nation-state also has its own individual character (*kokka no kosei*): that is, the nation-state also expresses its true character. As Nishida puts it, the nation-state "must be a world which has individual characters" (Nishida 2004c, 336), and hence "the polities of states cannot be exchangeable" (*ibid*). Here, we must pay attention to the fact that Nishida interprets the "national polity" (*kokutai*) —one of the most ideological concepts in modern Japan in relation to the Emperor-centred regime—as the individual character of the state. In particular, a pamphlet titled *Fundamentals of the National Polity* (*Kokutai no hongi*) was published in 1937, which glorified the national polity as the incomparable Japanese principle. Through his interpretation, Nishida might have tried to relativise the concept, which functioned as the absolute Imperial principle in the modern Japanese political context. For Nishida, the national polity is not a principle unique to the Japanese nation state, but each nation-state, which establishes the legal institutional system and mediates the contradiction, has its own "national polity" or its own individual character. In this context, *tekhnē* is the principle that establishes a state, which has an appropriate and rational "national polity" as the expression of its true individual character.

Thus far, we have seen how Nishida argues that *tekhnē* is necessary to establish the nation-state based on a culture. For Nishida, politics needs this *tekhnē*. He even claims that politics is *tekhnē*. Considering the argument we have developed so far, we should pay attention to the point that Nishida is convinced that the contradiction between *praxis* and *poiesis* does not cause any conflict or dispute or, to put it more precisely, any conflict or dispute would consequently be mediated by the totality. For Nishida, the aim of politics is to establish a nation-state where conflict or dispute does not occur and *tekhnē* is needed to establish the institutional system that removes any dispute or conflict by allocating an appropriate part to each individual. Nishida envisages culture as the totality that defines each individual as a subject to reproduce the world and this means that the particular part each individual plays as the subject can be culturally defined: the part of man, woman, student, teacher, father, mother, the Emperor… This is what Jacques Rancière calls the system of distribution of "police". He puts it thus:

> The police is thus first an order of bodies that defines the allocation of ways of doing, ways of being, and ways of saying, and sees that those bodies are assigned by name to a particular place and task; it is an order of the visible and the sayable that sees that a particular activity is visible and another is not, that this speech is understood as discourse and another as noise (Rancière 1999, 29).

In Nishida's discussion of the nation-state, *tekhnē* is used by politics to establish this "police" according to culture. As a result, the nation-state can be established as the system in which there is no dispute or conflict.

However, we should understand that the totality or the system of police may become possible by suppressing the conflict or dispute and culture may help to hide this suppression. In other words, it is possible that by arguing that culture can mediate the contradiction between *praxis* and *poiesis*, the nation-state tries to suppress dispute or conflict caused by the contradiction. Hence, we need to ask, in order to criticise and dissent from this possibility, what kind of strategy should be adopted? The answer to this question is very simple: that is, we should "agree" with Nishida's assumption that a totality like culture, which can mediate the contradiction, can emerge. Then, if we think that this mediation does not work adequately, we can protest that there is a gap between what the state argues and what we feel. Although the state argues that culture mediates the true individual characters we wish to express, we believe that cultural definitions of our true individual characters are actually not the true individual characters we want to express. In short, we can provoke "disagreement" and, thereby, we can create dispute or conflict caused by the apparent contradiction. This is "politics" in Rancière's sense. As Rancière argues, politics is the activity of identifying the point at which "disagreement" occurs and in order to evoke disagreement, there must be agreement. He puts it as follows:

> We should take disagreement to mean a determined kind of speech situation: one in which one of the interlocutors at once understands and does not understand what the other is saying. Disagreement is not the conflict between one who says white and another who says black. It is the conflict between one who says white and another who also says white but does not understand the same thing by it or does not understand that the other is saying the same thing in the name of whiteness (*ibid.*, x).

In short, disagreement occurs in the situation where the "interlocutors both understand and do not understand the same thing by the same words" (*ibid.*, xi). Thus, disagreement needs the agreement that they share the same thing and the same words and, in this sense, politics needs the shared or common concern.

From Rancière's point of view, Nishida's discussion on the nation-state establishes the field in which politics can occur through disagreement. Nevertheless, Nishida himself is convinced that existing cultures, such as the Japanese culture, can successfully mediate the contradiction and therefore that there is no possibility that the contradiction causes dispute or conflict. Nishida seems to ignore any possibility of conflict within culture. As a result, the nation-state which Nishida believes should be established according to *tekhnē* – this is the aim of Nishida's politics – eliminates politics. Nishida argues that politics is *tekhnē*, but this *tekhnē* as politics is the *tekhnē* to eliminate politics.

3. Japanese Culture and the Problem of the World New Order

As we have already seen, Nishida's theories could be developed to promote politics. This possibility was developed by several thinkers. For example, So In-shik, a journalist and thinker who actively published critiques from the 1930s to the 40s on the Korean Peninsula, discussed the possibility of the world order which was critical of Japanese colonial imperialism, under the strong influence of Nishida's philosophical logic.[1] Nishida's theory can thus be interpreted as an anti-imperialist theory of the world order and actually Nishida intended that his theory should be envisaged as such. According to Cho Kwanja, So envisaged a multi-centred world (*ta-chūshin no sekai*) that can mediate each individual equally. Such a perspective can be understood as the correlative of Nishida's discussion on culture as the mediation of the contradiction between *praxis* and *poiesis*. According to Nishida, through *praxis*, each individual tries to become the subject who creates order and this means that each individual strives to become the central subject. However, this attempt is only to be realised through *poiesis*, which produces the diversified or pluralistic world. As a result, each individual becomes the multi-centred subject mediated by culture. Thus, Nishida's theory underpins So's idea of a multi-centred world. Of course, So's intention was to criticise Japanese Imperialism, which caused the inequality and conflict between the coloniser and the colonised and Nishida's theory may also be seen as criticising Japanese Imperialism.

However, Nishida does not develop this possibility adequately because he envisages Japanese culture as the meta-centre, which can mediate the multi-centred world. Nishida claims that culture can mediate the contradiction and particularly, that Japanese culture can mediate the contradiction between each individual culture. In short, he believes that Japanese culture can operate as the meta-culture or as the meta-centre. Considering So's intention, this idea cannot be compatible with So's idea of the multi-centred world because, if Japanese culture were posited as the meta-culture, it would occupy the ultimate centre. In this sense, So's argument should be understood as the attempt to provoke disagreement with Nishida: they share the idea of a multi-centred world, but disagree on the point of whether Japanese culture could play the role of a meta-culture. In other words, So made politics work against Nishida.

Nishida's assumption of Japanese culture as the meta-culture/centre led to the vindication of the superiority of the Japanese national polity, which dismissed any chance of criticising the attempt to put the Japanese nation-state at the centre of a new order. In order to examine this problem, I shall first look at *The Problem of Japanese Culture* again and then examine "The Principle of the World New Order", written in 1943. According to Nishida, Japanese culture could play the role of mediating the East and the West. As he puts it:

In the Japanese spirit…the spirit of Oriental culture is made to live most fully, and at the same time it may possess something which can also combine directly with the spirit of…Western culture. In this sense a point of union between Eastern and Western culture can be sought in Japan. Further, therein perhaps we can foresee the future of history, which, as a contradictory self-identity… [2] (Nishida 2004b, 67).

According to Nishida, because Japan has adopted various cultures, "while it is said to be quick to take in and clever in understanding and adopting the cultures of various foreign countries, in ancient times, the cultures of China and India and after Meiji, Western culture, [Japan] is nonetheless spoken of as not [being] original"[3] (*ibid.*, 59). However, Nishida believes that this opinion cannot be validated. In other words, Nishida is convinced that "the Japanese have a way of seeing things and a way of thinking, peculiar to themselves and even while absorbing from Chinese and Indian cultures, the Japanese have come to create their own culture"[4] (*ibid.*), and, for Nishida, the peculiarity of Japanese culture is the receptiveness which can absorb any culture.

Because Japanese culture initially adopted Chinese and Indian cultures, it developed as Oriental culture. However, thanks to its receptiveness, Japanese culture could adopt Western culture after the Meiji Restoration and, consequently, it could fuse and mediate Oriental culture and Western culture. Thus, Japanese culture became the medium between Oriental and Western cultures and, in this sense, Nishida is convinced that Japanese culture could play the role of a world culture (*sekai-bunka*) as a meta-culture. Here we understand that this meta-culture is the same as the meta-centre. This is the reason why he believes in the superiority of the Japanese national polity. As we have seen in the last section, Nishida regards the national polity as the individual character of the nation-state and the nation-state is established by *tekhnē* to ensure culture. Therefore, he believes the quality of the national polity also reflects the culture on which the nation-state is based and is convinced that the Japanese national polity, reflecting Japanese culture as the mediator between Oriental and Western cultures, has to be superior to any other culture. Predictably, Nishida argues that the Japanese nation-state has to take the initiative of making the Co-prosperity Sphere and the World New Order: the new world order in which each nation-state can be mediated and express its own individual character. In fact, this is the main argument in "The Principle of the World New Order".

In "The Principle of the World New Order" Nishida argues that the current ideal of the new world order is underpinned by the collusion between ethno-centrism and abstract cosmopolitanism. It is envisaged and promoted by the strong countries (that is, Western countries) and suppresses or ignores the concrete perspective of the world of Asian people, who were colonised as the result of Western imperialism. Thus criticising the current situation underpinned by Western imperialistic logic, Nishida argues that it is necessary to envisage a new world order, which respects the individuality of each nation, including Asian people. The war (he claims) demonstrated that the world order is in a state of crisis in which principles such as Wilsonian idealism cannot work adequately anymore. Nishida states:

> To say that each state or nation, by transcending itself, constructs a single world is not, as in the Wilsonian League of Nations, merely to advocate the self-determination of people whereby each nation's independence is recognised equally. Such a world is nothing more than the eighteenth-century abstract world ideology. The present Great World War is demonstrating that the solution to today's actual historical problem is impossible in terms of that ideology [5] (Nishida 2005, 445).

Therefore, Nishida believes that the new world order has to be general in the true sense: it has to be accepted by both Western and Asian people so that no one will be suppressed. In this new world order, each regional or local culture, as the basis of each nation-state, has to be upheld and each nation-state can thereby express its own individual character: their own "national polity". Nishida believes that such a new world order could be established only by referring to the world culture and that only Japan could play the central role in such a mission. From this standpoint, the aim of the establishment of the Co-prosperity Sphere is also reinterpreted as the creation of a new world order based on a world culture. After arguing that the "fundamental principle of the world new order" is "being demanded by today's Great World War" (*ibid.*, 445), Nishida states:

If the problem of today's Great World War is as stated above–and the basic principle of a new world order is also as I have stated–then the basic principle of the East Asia Co-prosperity Sphere must naturally emerge from this as well. In the past, because of the imperialism of European nations, the East Asian nations have been oppressed and colonised, and their own world historical missions have been wrested from them. Now the various nations of East Asia must awaken to their own world-historical mission as East Asian nations: they must all transcend themselves and construct their own distinct world, thereby achieving their own world-historical mission as East Asian nations. This is the basic principle of the construction of the East Asia Co-prosperity Sphere…for such a particular world to be constructed, there must be that which becomes its centre and undertakes its task. In East Asia today, that centre is none other than our country, Japan … today's East Asian War deciding the direction of world history for future generations [6] (*ibid.*, 446).

In short, Nishida argues that the war had to become the moment to establish the Co-prosperity Sphere where East Asian nations anticipated the realisation of the new world order and that Japan, which is a nation-state based on Japanese culture as the world culture, has to take the initiative to establish such an order.

Thus, Nishida states that Japan has to constitute itself as the subject to spread the principle of a world culture embodied in the Japanese national polity.

The fundamental policy of the intellectual guidance, learning, and education of our nation must be grounded thoroughly and deeply in the underlying principle of our National Polity, and it must be founded in a grasp of historical reality and by the principle for forming the World as worlds. The reason we must reject the Anglo-American thought is that it derives from imperialism, whereby, with a sense of the Anglo-American people's own superiority, it views East Asia as its colony [7] (*ibid.*, 447).

Nishida argues that the principle embodied in the Japanese national polity has to be spread by Japan as the principle to establish the new world order. Here, Nishida rephrases the new world order as the "World as worlds" (*Sekai-teki sekai*). By this Nishida attempts to describe the new world order as a totalised world which mediates each state or culture as a small, particular world.

Thus far, we have examined how Nishida discusses Japanese culture in a wartime context. From the angle of the proponents of Nishida's semantic tug of war, these discussions can be understood as a criticism of the gap between the ideal of the Co-prosperity Sphere and the reality of the war waged in the name of the Co-prosperity Sphere. Proponents argue that, even if Nishida glorifies the "Imperial House" (*Kōshitsu*) and the "Imperial Way" (*Kōdō*) as the "principle of world formation" (*ibid.*, 446-447), they have to dissent from the wartime ideology. However, even if this understanding is correct, Nishida's discussion inevitably involves a paradox: to establish a normative perspective which criticises the imperialistic conduct of the Japanese Empire he endorses the ontological and historical narrative which justifies Japan as an imperialist empire.

Nishida's logic clearly lacks the possibility of criticising the trajectory which led to the present status of the Japanese Empire as an imperialist nation-state. For Nishida, Japanese culture has succeeded in mediating any conflicts and the presence of the "Imperial House" and the unbroken lineage of the Emperor has to be understood as the evidence of the successful history of Japanese culture. Nishida thinks that this is the distinctive characteristic of Japanese culture and he can therefore argue that only Japanese culture can play the role of a meta-centre or meta-culture, which can mediate each culture at each centre. Although Nishida is critical of Japanese imperialistic conduct during the war, by idealising Japanese culture, he suppresses the conflicts which should have occurred through Japanese imperialism as the process of Japanese modernisation and thereby eliminates politics within the Japanese Empire. Thus, Nishida cannot maintain a critical standpoint towards Japanese colonialism as the history of the Japanese Empire. This point becomes seriously problematic when we consider the continuity between Japanese colonial imperialism and the Japanese invasion of East Asian countries during the Asia Pacific War. This is because there is the possibility that this paradox could resonate with justification of the invasion as emancipation.

Conclusion: How to Dissent from Depoliticisation?

As we have seen above, Nishida developed the logic of eliminating politics or depoliticisation. What could Nishida have done to avoid this logic and criticise Japanese imperialism more thoroughly? We have already seen the answer to this question. Nishida did not have to abandon his assumption that a totality like culture, which can mediate the contradiction, can emerge, but he should have argued that, despite Japanese culture, the Japanese Empire has never succeeded in mediating the conflicts between the coloniser and the colonised, or between Japan and others. This would be a way to radicalise Nishida's philosophy and thereby enhance the possibility of the politicisation of his philosophy.

(Endnotes)
1) On the detail of So In-shik's arguments, see Cho Kwanja (2007).
2) I have adapted the translation in Tsunoda et al (1958, 872).
3) I have cited the translation from *ibid.*, 869.
4) I have cited the translation from *ibid.*
5) I have adapted the translation in Dilworth et al (1998, 74).
6) I have adapted the translation in *ibid.*, 74.
7) I have adapted the translation in *ibid.*

References
Cho, Kwanja. 2007. *Shokumin-chi chōsen teikoku nihon no bunka-renkan: Nashonarizumu to hanpuku-suru shokuminchi-shugi* [The Cultural Linkage between Colonial Korea and Imperial Japan: Nationalism and Repeating Colonialism]. Tokyo: Yūshisha.
Dilworth, David A. and Valdo H. Viglielmo with Agustin Jacinto Zavala, eds. and trans. 1998. *Sourcebook for Modern Japanese Philosophy: Selected Documents*. Westport: Greenwood Press.
Monbu-sho, ed. 1937. *Kokutai no hongi* [Fundamentals of the National Polity]. Tokyo: Naikaku-insatsukyoku hakkoka.
Nishida, Kitarō. 2004a. Poieshisu to purakushisu [Poiesis and Praxis]. In *Shinban Nishida Kitarō Zenshū* [New Edition Complete Collection of Nishida Kitaro]. 9: 191-231. Tokyo: Iwanami Shoten.
Nishida, Kitarō. 2004b. Nihon bunka no mondai [The Problem of Japanese Culture]. In *Shinban Nishida Kitarō Zenshū* IX [New Edition Complete Collection of Nishida Kitaro]. 9: 1-85. Tokyo: Iwanami Shoten.
Nishida, Kitarō. 2004c. Kokka-riyū no mondai [The Problem of Reason of State]. In *Shinban Nishida Kitarō Zenshū* [New Edition Complete Collection of Nishida Kitaro]. 9: 301-356. Tokyo: Iwanami Shoten.
Nishida, Kitarō. 2005. Sekai shin-chitsujo no genri [The Principle of the World New Order]. In *Shinban Nishida Kitarō Zenshū* [New Edition Complete Collection of Nishida Kitaro]. 11: 444-450. Tokyo: Iwanami Shoten.
Nishitani, Keiji. 1979. Kindai no chōkoku shiron [My Personal View of Overcoming Modernity]. In *Kindai no chōkoku* [Overcoming Modernity]. Ed. Yoshimi Takeuchi, 18-37. Tokyo: Fuzanbō.
Rancière, Jacques. 1999. *Disagreement: Politics and Philosophy*. Minneapolis: University of Minnesota Press.

Takeuchi, Yoshimi. 1979. Kindai no chōkoku [Overcoming Modernity]. In *Kindai no chōkoku* [Overcoming Modernity]. Ed Yoshimi Takeuchi, 273-341. Tokyo: Fuzanbō.

Tsunoda, Ryusaku, William Theodore de Barry and Donald Keene eds. 1958. *Sources of Japanese Tradition*. New York: Columbia University Press.

Ueda, Shizuteru. 1995. Nishida Kitatrō: "Ano sensō" to "nihon bunka no mondai" [Nishida Kitaro: The War and the Problem of Japanese Culture]. *Shisō* 857: 107-133.

Yamada, Munemutsu. 1975. *Showa no seishin-shi: Kyoto gakuha no tetsugaku* [The History of the Spirit of Showa: The Philosophy of Kyoto School]. Kyoto: Jinbun shoin.

[Symposium]
Reading the Kyoto School Philosophy as a Non-Western Discourse:
Contingency, Nothingness, and the Public

Kosuke SHIMIZU
Department of Global Studies
Ryukoku University

Introduction

The Kyoto School philosophy was allegedly the world level existentialism, and had an enormous impact on religious philosophy in the post-war era in the East and West. Nishida Kitaro's concepts such as 'place of nothingness' and 'eternal present' are conspicuously the main philosophical focal point in this context, and they represent a transcending state of mind based on the Buddhist philosophy. Despite the world level quality of philosophy, there is a dark-side in their history however, and this is particularly important in the context of international relations as an academic discipline (IR) as it provides a cautionary tale for those engaging in the 'non-Western' thought.

The story of the Kyoto School shows ambiguous and sometimes hazardous relations between philosophy and power politics, international and imperial, theory and practice, abstract and reality, and the symbolic and the real. What is at stake here is the applicability of philosophical idea of international orders to the politics of power relations and violence. It is in the case of Nishida's philosophy of nothingness in the WWII that the confrontation between philosophy and power politics comes to the fore. While Nishida contended that his philosophy on the basis of 'place of nothingness', which was presumably tolerant to 'others' thus inherently multicultural on the abstract level of contemplation, was supposedly reified in Japan, Japan as a nation-state in reality and substantive politics shamelessly invaded other nations in Asia with brutal violence in the name of the struggle against the domination of the West (Shimizu 2011).

The gap between Japan on the basis of his philosophy and Japan of nation-state, thus pragmatic power politics, is closely related to what Sakai (2007) calls international order and imperial order. He explains that the international order here means the relationship among the 'civilized' nations which guarantees the equal membership and the principle of non-intervention to other nation's domestic affairs. On the other hand, the imperial order is an order with which the 'civilized' nations control and exploit the less civilized areas by means of violence. While these orders were supposed to reside in the different areas, thus removed from each other in the context of the Western IR, they are different sides of the same coin (Sakai 2007, 6). This is precisely the moment Suzuki (2009) tried to explain. Suzuki argues, in criticizing the English School's Euro-centered perception towards the International Society, that the English School scholars 'do not sufficiently acknowledge the fact that European imperialism was at its height when the Society expanded to East Asia and to date they have not adequately considered the possibility that both (Japanese and Chinese) states may have been exposed to the darker side of the Society' (Suzuki 2009, loc. 525). This darker side of the order is also taken up, although on a different level of analysis, by Hannah Arendt in the name of the dichotomy between the public and private. According to Arendt, the public, which is consisted of the equal rational members for speech, becomes possible only when their private lives are supported by slavery, of which she thinks inherently violent. This violence is pre-political supposed to reside 'outside the *polis*', thus despotic (Arendt 1958, 26) but in fact one cannot exist without the other. As a result, when the international order becomes instable, this is called 'crisis' from the West, but an emergence of a 'new world order' from the rest (Kosaka et.al. 1943, 11), while the imperial order is always 'crisis' for the colonized areas.

This paper strives to clarify the reason of the Kyoto School's, Nishida's in particular, involvement in the wartime regime and draw a cautionary tale for the contemporary non-Western IRT with special attention to the two orders Sakai, Suzuki, and Arendt referred to. The primary theme to address here is the influence of the two orders onto Nishida's political action. This inevitably leads us to the question of language, particularly 'Japan' in the context of the international and imperial orders before and during the WWII. It is also important here to investigate how they attempted to philosophically evade the influence of, and transcend, the prevailing two orders.

In order to answer these questions, this paper starts with an explanation of the backdrops of the non-Western IRT and its similarities to the political involvement of Kyoto School philosophy. What we concentrate upon in this context is the backdrops of their emergence, particularly the domination of the West over the other areas, the decline of the world hegemony, and destabilization of international order. Secondly, a brief explanation of the Kyoto School's philosophy will be introduced. Here, I will explain why the philosophy of the Kyoto School is accepted widely ranging from pure logics to history, science, and religion. Thirdly, I will focus upon Kyoto School's political philosophy and discourses on history and culture on the basis of 'place of nothingness' and 'eternal present'. This is because their political contentions directly related to their involvement in the military government were mainly found in their historical and cultural writings. Fourth, the relationship between Kyoto School's abstract concepts regarding Japan as a distinct culture, such as 'place of nothingness' and the 'eternal present', and Japan as a nation-state will be analyzed. By this, I will try to draw the cautionary tales from the Kyoto School's experience to the contemporary non-Western IRT literature.

Non-Western IRT, the National Schools, and the Structural Changes in World Affairs

Kyoto School philosophy has recently come to be seen as one of the sources of the original formulation of international relations (IR). Chris Goto-Jones's prominent work on Nishida's philosophy (Goto-Jones 2005) and Graham Gerald Ong's application of "emptiness" to IR theory (Ong 2004) are good examples. Chih-Yu Shih's examination of Nishida's philosophy is also worth noting here as it attempts to put Nishida's "place of nothingness" into the context of contemporary IR (Shih 2012).

Although their understanding and explication of Kyoto School philosophy in contemporary IR are remarkable, what is commonly missing in these works is the contextualization of the Kyoto School politics. Historical contextualization of the School is essential in accommodating Kyoto School philosophy into the contemporary international relations discourse as it clearly unveils the ambiguous relations between the international and the imperial.

This task is extremely imperative in contemporary IR which can be characterized by the emergence of the non-Western national 'Schools' such as Chinese, Korean and Japanese Schools (Cho 2013). It seems that there are some common aspects in the Kyoto School and those national 'Schools'. For instance, both the Kyoto School and the contemporary national schools develop discourses of the world on the basis of nation-based perception towards culture. Like the philosophy of world history by the Kyoto School philosophers, those national schools frequently refer to cultural distinctiveness of their nations such as a long history of their nations, and often employ abstract concepts of ideal state of affairs. Both also forcibly insist that this ideal state of affairs should be applied to the international context, and will lead to the stable and enduring global order. What underlying here is an assumption that the world is becoming unstable largely because of the rapid restructuring process of prevailing order as the hegemon looses its power over the rest of the world. They also contend that the reason of the instability is because of the limitation of the Western modernity and rationalism, which should be replaced by the Eastern convention and political thought. In fact, Nishida's philosophy has often been interpreted as a "post-modern" discourse (Araya 2008, 10), and regularly referred to an attempt to 'transcend' Western intellectual deficiencies same as contemporary non-Western IRT discourses striving to provide an alternative to Western IRT. Thus revealing and clarifying the reason why the mainstream Kyoto School philosophers were involved in the wartime regime will benefit the non-Western literature of IR in the present by unveiling the hidden risks and dangers the literature might involve.

Contemporary international relations as an academic discipline is, as I explained in the introduction, characterized by the emergence of non-Western IRT literature. In this context, the perception criticizing Western modernization and civilization in non-Western areas, which is exclusively materialized in terms of appearance rather than philosophical principles, permeates the literature. Thus modernization and civilization in the 'rest' of the world ostensibly took place in the form of physical objects such as buildings, roads, and airports as well as Western concepts through the introduction of such institutions as political representation and the market economy (Khatab 2011; Nakano 2011). In this sense, the technologies and sciences introduced to the non-Western societies in the name of civilizational development were exclusively instrumental in its orientation. The importation of instrumental technology led many non-Western scholars to put an emphasis on different soul, spirit, culture, and history of the non-West, which supposedly have inherent characteristics distinct from Western civilization (Kang 2007; Zhao 2012).

The adherence of the scholars to the difference of the non-Western nations and regions from the Western civilization is closely related to the ontological perception towards the world. Because non-Western nations, and Asian nations in particular, have allegedly different and indigenous cultures and histories, they have a unique ontology of world affairs. One example of such non- or anti-Western ontology is the "Chinese School" discourse, which places a special emphasis on the tributary system (Kang 2007, 2010), a system of ancient Chinese governance (Zhao 2006, Yan 2011) or the Chinese concept of relationality, *guanxi* (Qin 2010, 2011). There are many who are currently engaging with this new academic enterprise of the Chinese version of international relations; the most influential among them is Zhao Tingyang, who recently developed the theory of *tianxia*. *Tianxia* is the traditional Chinese concept of 'the world all under heaven' (Zhao 2012, Yan 2011). By applying this ancient Chinese concept to contemporary international affairs, his framework comes close to what is traditionally called World Society theory in that it transcends the borders of nation-states (Buzan 2004, xviii). *Tianxia* embraces all people and communities 'under heaven' as there is no concept of foreign countries, but they are 'theoretically taken-in sub-states' (Zhao 2006, 35). This is because Zhao's interpretation of Chinese philosophy is based on a specific ontology of 'relations' rather than individual agents (Zhao 2006, 33). This relationality, which will be touched upon shortly, is the reason why the Chinese political system focuses more on social order than on individuals, the main ontological subject of Western philosophy.

Their articulation of world order is not just theoretical but always practical because, as Zhao contends, theory in this context is not just about what is but also about what is expected (Zhao 2006, 30). In this way, their perception and interpretation of the world is tremendously different from Western international relations, and they insist that this different perception of China should form the core of the future of world affairs.

A similar argument can be found in David Kang's assertion that there was a long-lasting peace under the Chinese tributary system from the fourteenth to the nineteenth century. He argues that East Asia had enjoyed peace and order before the violent arrival of Western imperialism. In contrast to the Westphalian system of interstate relations, which was defined by its formal equality and incessant interstate conflict, the East Asian tributary system was characterized by formal inequality and 'centuries of stability among the core participants' (Kang 2010, 201/5803). This logic is closely connected with a Sinocentric view, asserting that what is good for China is good for East Asia, and when China is strong and stable, order has been preserved (Kang 2007, 201; Callahan 2012, 41).

Qin Yaqing (2011) focuses on the context of *guanxi*, relationality. He argues that Asian international relations are better explained by relationality than by formal rules and institutions. Qin illustrates Western individualism as 'bundles of rice straws in the paddy fields,' while he describes the Chinese social structure as 'continuous circles of ripples on the lake' each of which 'is connected in one way or another' (Qin 2009, 7-8).

What permeates their non-Western version of international relations theories is the persistent contradiction in their arguments between the purpose of transcending the Westphalia system and their insistence on a Sinocentric formulation of future IR. They are understandably enthusiastic in criticizing the violent character of Western modernity, which can be divided into the international and imperial order, but they articulate an allegedly new system of world order based on *tianxia* as a superior system to the Westphalian order, on top of which China, as the rising nation-state, implicitly resides. In this sense, their version of international relations theory shows little difference from Japan's Greater East Asian Co-Prosperity Area (Chen 2012, 477). In fact, the concept of *tianxia* comes close to Nishida Kitaro's theory of world history, which was later deployed by Japan's imperialist government for the justification of their invasion over the Asian continent (Nishida 1950a; Shimizu 2011).

What is underlying here is the concept of inclusiveness that both theories claim to have. It is an open system for all nations and cultures. They were designed to be multicultural from the beginning of their theoretical articulation. For the sake of multiculturalism, they see the nation-state as the main obstacle to the application of their theories to the practical politics. In fact, they both cast doubt on the concept of the nation-state claiming that it is a product of Western civilization. Consequently they try to provide a different framework of governance for Asian (Nishida 1950a; Zhao 2006).

However, the story does not stop here. Both of the theories rely on the concept of nations, China in the case of the Chinese School and Japan in the case of the Kyoto School as subject in depicting the future world order, despite their critical perception towards the Westphalian system. In fact, both theories are based on a presumption of hierarchal order, and their nations are granted sole responsibility to maintain order (Nishida 1950b; Zhao 2006). Although we have to wait and see in the case of the Chinese School, the Nishida's case resulted in a tragedy in which the subtle and somehow ambiguous balance between multiculturalism and Japan's role as a supposed leader of the region in the Nishida's discourse of world history was completely destroyed by the military government as the latter overwhelmed the former. As a result, Nishida was regarded as an apologist for Japan's war against the West in the post-War era, despite his initial intention to contribute to the world peace (Shimizu 2011).

This contradiction between the idealized harmonious future world without borders and the powerful influence of the concept of the nation-state over scholars' perceptions is not limited to the Chinese School. The alleged "Japanese School" (Chen 2012) and the "Korean School" (Cho 2013) are no exception. Because they articulate the world in terms of the nation-state, despite their enthusiastic engagement in renewing IR, they take the West as their only reference point (Chen 2012, 477). This means that the discourses of non-Western IRT should be understood in the context of unceasing confrontations and incessant competition among nation-states.

The Kyoto School Philosophy, Place of Nothingness, and Eternal Present

While the political meanings and political consequences of the emergence of the Chinese School are still unclear, the Kyoto School's case is by no means ambiguous. They supported the military government and provided the justification for Japan's aggression over the Asian continent. In order to comprehend the reason of their involvement, it is imperative to investigate the philosophy of the Kyoto School. Nishida Kitaro was the prominent philosopher of the School, and his philosophy has been analyzed and interpreted differently by scholars of various disciplines. Among those, religious philosophy has been the main academic body. Some of them argue that the philosophy of the School is exclusively Eastern, while some contend that Nishida's philosophy is hybrid in a sense that it is based on the Western philosophy in conjunction with Buddhist thoughts (Arisaka 1997, 546). In any case, those analyze the philosophical discourses of the Kyoto School from religious studies equate them with some sort of mysticism (Kosaka 2008).

While these mainstream arguments of the Kyoto School regularly focus on such concepts as 'pure experience' and 'place of nothingness', recent Japanese literature on Nishida tends to focus on Nishida's concept of time (Nishizuka 2010; Kobayashi 2013). As in the case of literature of the Kyoto School in general, IR literature of non-Western thought has hardly focused on the concept of time. This is partly because the concept of time does not appear in Nishida's early writings, such as *the Inquiry into the Good*, which most IR researchers of the Kyoto School rely on in their investigations, and partly because Nishida himself did not put much emphasis on this concept in his political writings even in his later years.

So, what is time in Nishida's philosophy? Time is obviously a confusing concept. Nishida argues that the present is eternal and will never be past or future; it is neither determined by past incidents nor controlled by future plans. Time is generated in the form of the self-determination of the eternal present. It appears ubiquitously and disappears everywhere (Nishida 1948, 342, Nishizuka 2010, 107-8). Therefore, Nishida's concept of the eternal present appears to have a remarkable discontinuity from the past and the future. Nevertheless, time appears continuous from the past through the present to the future in the form of history. As a result, Nishida defines time as the "continuity of the discontinuity" (Nishida 1948, 342).

The definition of time as the "continuity of the discontinuity" is in no way easy to comprehend. He began his philosophy with the concept of "pure experience" and later developed it into the "place of nothingness". In the later years, his focus was shifted as far as to the "eternal present." It appears that his philosophy encountered some discontinuities during his philosophical life. What is imperative in Nishida's thought on time is that the present appears in the form of discontinuity, and this is open to coincidentality. What characterizes his thought here is Nishida's relentless pursuit of openness to others and his willingness to accept the coincidentality. The "eternal present" is, by definition, remote from the past or present, and is never controlled or determined by them. This means that the present is open to anything unexpected, thus ready for coincidence. Thus the present is presumably inclusive for anything while exposed to anything. In other words, it is the moment in which the "pure experience" takes place, and this is the core of his multiculturalist discourse.

Obviously this concept of time may appear to the audience of the School as forming an indispensable contradiction with his political writings, which many Kyoto School researchers regard as conservative and nationalistic. If he was willing to develop such an open-minded and multiculturalist philosophy of inclusivity, how could Nishida have become an advocate of Japan's imperial and expansionist government? The military expansion of Japan was clearly exercised on the basis of a planned strategy, and this surely meant the present was controlled by the future for becoming a member of the international order while limited by the past of the violent imperial order of the West exploiting the rest of the world. Thus his political involvement in the wartime regime can only be understood in the context that his political writings were exclusively prescriptive mainly craving for the expansion of the international society to the rest of the world without power relations among the member nation-states. For him, this becomes only possible when the expansion is put into practice by non-violent means. In other words, he intended to change the course of the Japan's violent military expansion policies to a more inclusive and multicultural foreign policies by giving new meanings to the war slogans such as 'Eight Corners under One Roof' (Yoshida 2011, 17).

That his political contention was exclusively prescriptive means that he perceived that the contemporary world was far from what his thought to be the ideal. His description of the new world order shows his concern about the inequality among the member states in the contemporary international order. To him, the international order was anything but what the English School considers to be present in the form of International Society. It was rather violent and exploitative. Thus what Nishida considered to be present internationally throughout his life was the imperial order of the West, and it can be said that he tried to put it back into the order among equal sovereign states with his concept of the eternal present.

Transcending the International

In order to transcend the imperial order and establish a truly international sphere consisting of equal members, there must be some one who takes charge of and carry out this change, Nishida contends. Nishida and his disciples focused on the concepts of history and culture of Japan in this context. The reasons why they were convinced that Japan was to take responsibility can be derived partly from their understandings of the self-definition of Japanese as non-European, the victory of over Russia in 1905, the unprecedented pace of the rapid civilization. But what is more important, in Nishida's case, is a perception that Japan is a reification of place of nothingness.

What characterizes the world order on the basis of nothingness is relationality. In the Western IR based on state sovereignty presumes independent and pre-given subjectivity. Nation-state in this context is assumed to exist before the interactions among them take place. On the other hand, in the case of the perception based upon relationality, nation-state is constituted through the relations. Thus nation in this context is constructed every moment, the eternal present.

However, the place of nothingness does not have definite substantive pre-given existence. What constitutes this alleged place of nothingness is continuity of discontinuity. Nishida contends that it is in the imperial household (Nishida 1950b).

> In the case of Japanese national polity, the imperial household is the beginning and the end of the world. The imperial household embraces the past and future, it becomes the center of evolution as the self-determination of the eternal present, and this is the quintessence of Japan's national polity (Nishida 1950c, 409)

The imperial household is in this way supposed to prove Japan to be continuity of discontinuities.

The place of nothingness in the world history appears in the form of concentric circles. The world therefore consists of a number of concentric circles and the world itself appears in this mapping as a larger concentric circle which embraces all. In this mapping the concentric circles has not clear boundaries, which makes sharp contrast with the Westphalian system based on the principle of mutual exclusion. This overlaps what Qin Yaqing (2011) calls 'ripples' which I introduced previously, and this perception towards the contemporary world comes close to the *tianxia* system of ancient China. In fact, Nishida and his disciples often referred to the *tianxia* system as one of the ideal models of the world order of the next generation (Nishida 1950e; Kosaka et.al. 1943, 340-341).

The Kyoto School philosophers contend that the concept of Great East Asian Co-prosperity Sphere (GEACS), which has been commonly understood in the post-war era, as the justification for Japan's imperialist territorial expansion, should be the reification of world system of place of nothingness. This system makes sharp contrast with the Westphalian system, according to the Kyoto School philosophers, in that the former is based on morality while the latter on instrumental reason. This is the reason why the GEACS is morally superior to the imperialists in the West.

But what guarantees the moral superiority of the GEACS? They contend that the morality in the contemporary world resides in the human function to materialize the world history. Human beings are born in the history and, in turn, create it. Individuals are destined to perform the crucial role of world creation, and we should make effort to complete this mission. Although there are some varieties in the interpretation of morality and human existence among the Kyoto School philosophers, the simplest interpretation of it states that most imperative aspect of human beings in the world history is 'obedience' (Koyama 2001). The obedience in this context should not be comprehended in the way that it is frequently used in the contemporary IR. It is far from despotism or totalitarianism. Rather it is obedience to the nothingness. Thus, the Kyoto School philosophers firmly believed that the Western morality is based on being while Japan's morality is on the concept of nothingness, and this is the key to transcend the international order prevailing in the world of imperialism.

In both cases of Nishida and his disciples, it was clear that what they strived to do was to hijack the meanings of the concepts frequently used in the discourses of direct total war between Japan and the Wes in varying degrees. The result was unfortunately the failure. Their discourses never achieved the initial goal. So what went wrong?

The Cautionary Tale of the Kyoto School

Nishida's effort to highjack the foreign relations of Japan and to change its course to a more harmonious and peaceful world ended in disastrous failure, so did his disciples'. An article Nishida wrote specifically for Prime Minister Tojo's speech of the Great East Asian Co-prosperity Declaration was substantially edited without Nishida's permission and used in the speech in order solely to justify the aggression of the Japanese army over the Asian continent. Nishida was extremely disappointed to hear Tojo's speech and later died in sorrow. The reputation of Nishida as well as his disciples is marred even now, and they are generally regarded as an intellectual war criminal. So what sort of possible explanation can we find?

One possible explanation can be found in Kobayashi's analysis of Nishida's personality (Kobayashi 2011). Kobayashi argues that it was unexceptional to have much admiration for the emperor among the Japanese of Nishida's generation, and Nishida was apparently no exception. It was his adherence to the Emperor system, Kobayashi maintains, that gave him the reason to write the draft (Kobayashi 2011, 335-356). In fact, there are numerous writings of Nishida's on the emperor and his predecessors, which prove his extraordinary attachment to the emperor.

But there is another reason for his exclusive focus on the Emperor system in the political writings. Nishida believed that the unbroken line of the imperial household had a symbolic existence, and this resonated with his philosophy of the "place of nothingness" and the "eternal present." The "place of nothingness" does not have any shape or frame before it is established by definition. It is like a container without any boundaries or walls. In this sense, the "place of nothingness" can hardly have its continuous identity. On the other hand, the "eternal present" is the continuity of discontinuities. If the concept of time is inherently discontinuous, how could one maintain his/her identity? This is a question, which unceasingly annoyed Nishida throughout his life.

If the something same takes place every discontinuous moment, the place of nothingness does have a shape, though it is only in a retrospective sense. This is the unbroken line of the imperial household of Japan. Japan in fact absorbed numerous cultures from abroad in many aspects including philosophy, thoughts, religion, technology, and science. Nishida considered

Japan's history of absorption and the imperial household that guarantee Japan's character of the "place of nothingness" (Nishida 1950b).

However, his configuration of the world of place of nothingness with the imperial household residing the center of it was too naïve. Nishida's philosophical conceptualization of harmonious world was easily exploited by the harsh reality of power politics and abused in justifying the imperialist aggression of Japanese military. The emperor was by no means the representation of nothingness or the core of Japan's muliticuluralist identity as Nishida presumed. The emperor was in fact the representation of being, being of an aggressive sort in Japanese politics of the time (Kobayashi 2011, 341). The emperor represented the reification of the nation-state of Japan, which was naturally constructed upon the notion of the legitimate use of violence granted by the imperial order. Ironically, one could suggest that Nishida's articulation of the emperor was materialized in the form of the imperial household of the post-war period as a symbolic existence without political power (Kobayashi 2011, 341).

Another possible reason of their failure resides in epistemology. While the philosophers of the School contended that Japan is a reification of place of nothingness, thus should become the leader of the next world order on the basis of morality rather than instrumental reason, the reality of Japan was far from matching that expectation. Inoue Toshikazu (2011) argues that Japan during the twenty years' crisis was far from traditional society constructed upon morality. It rather showed a typical representation of consumer society, which comes close to what Arendt (1958) and Fromme (195?) saw in Germany before the advent of Nazism. There are also numerous diaries and letters the Kyoto School philosopher wrote which indeed show how they were disturbed by the prevailing consumerism in Japan. Thus, in order to understand the failure of their political enterprise, we cannot miss the way they perceived the world, an epistemological question.

This is an emblematic misperception that the world could be understood in a dichotomized way. The Kyoto School philosophers were too much concentrated on the West/East division, and never cast a sufficient light to 'in-between', despite their extraordinary emphasis on the relationality of subjects. This is typical in configuring international relations, particularly when we are driven to see it in a confrontational way. In other words, their perception towards the world was not based on the place of nothingness. It was rather the Western modernism that they relied upon in depicting the twenty years' of crisis. If they made possible to stick to the idea of the place of nothingness and eternal present, they could have become aware that such dichotomies as West/East and US/Japan are themselves human construct and far from essential and pre-given existence. In other words, these dichotomies were already institutionalized in their discourses, and not open to contingencies, which might have changed their political perceptions. Their discourses were totally self-contained and had no rooms for coincidentality or different interpretations to take place. Thus it is safely to say here that their narratives were indeed very much Western oriented to universalism in terms of their perception and assumptions, and set of subjectivities. In fact, some critical readings of the school frequently insist that the Kyoto School philosophy should be interpreted as an extension of Western philosophy and an attempt to 'pierce' it to transcend (Sakai and Isomae 2010, 23-27). In this context, their effort was not sufficient to achieve that goal. This interpretation is imperative in the context of political engagement of the School as it shows that the School effort was incomplete and stopped at the level of universalism in the particularistic disguise.

What can we say about the non-Western IRT literature based on our understanding of the Kyoto School's experience? First, the notions of inclusivity and openness are definitely the goals to pursue. However, it is definitely naïve to say that simply introducing different concepts and ideas on the abstract level will materialize these norms in the substantive world automatically. As Nishida and his disciples' experience suggests, knowledge and intellect are always in danger of abuse by the prevailing power. It seems particularly so when the romantic ideas of peace and inclusivity are articulated in defense of a particular and present nation-state. Nevertheless we are obliged to pursue norms and prescriptions, because, as E. H. Carr suggests, norms and morals are indispensable aspects of international relations (Carr 1946). What we need to do here is to construct a concrete programme for materializing the ideal state of affairs. Without them, the discourses will be abused by the power politics. In order to avoid this, we have to balance the realist and utopian understandings of world affairs.

A paper presented at WISC Frankfurt 2014. Work in progress. Please do not cite without the permission of the author.

Notes
1) Economic Development and Democratization: Backdrops of the Kyoto School
2) Place of Nothingness and Philosophy of Emptiness: Philosophical foundation
3) Kyoto School's Involvement in the War and their Political Philosophy: Their Relations to the Navy
4) Culture and Nation-State: Theory and Practice in the Kyoto School's Case

References
Araya, Daisuke. (2008)*Nishida Kitaro: Rekishi no Ronrigaku* [Nishida Kitaro: The Logic of History]. Tokyo: Kodansha.
Arisaka, Yoko (1997), 'Beyond "East and West" Nishida's Universalism and Postcolonial Critique', *The Review of Politics*, 59 (3), 541-560.
Arendt, Hannah (1990)'Philosophy and Politics', *Social Research* 57 (1)73-103.
Buzan, Barry. (2004), *From International to World Society?: English School Theory and the Social Structure of Globalisation*, Cambridge: Cambridge University Press.
Callahan, William A. (2012), "Sino-Speak: Chinese Exceptionalism and the Politics of History", *The Journal of Asian Studies*, 71 (1), 33-55.
Carr, E. H. (1946)*The Twenty Years' Crisis: 1919-1939*, second edition, London: Macmillan.
Chen, Ching-Chang. (2012), 'The Im/possibility of Building Indigenous Theories in a Hegemonic Discipline: The Case of Japanese International Relations', Asian Perspective, 36 (3), pp.463-492.
Cho, Young Chul (2013), "Colonialism and Imperialism in the Quest for a Universalist Korean-Style International Relations Theory, *Cambridge Review of International Affairs*, available on-line http://www.tandfonline.com/doi/abs/10.1080/09557571.2013.807425#.Uu3yyfbmZjc (2/2/2014 Access)
Goto-Jones, Chris. (2005)*Political Philosophy in Japan: Nishida, the Kyoto School, and Co-Prosperity*. London: Routledge.
Heisig, James W. (2001)*Philosophers of Nothingness: An Essay on the Kyoto School*. Honolulu: Hawaii University Press.
Kang, David C. (2007), *China Rising: Peace, Power and Order in East Asia*, New York: Columbia University Press.
Kang, David C. (2010), *East Asia Before the West: Five Centuries of Trade and Tribute*, New York: Columbia University Press.
Khatab, Sayed (2011), "International Relations of Modernity in Sayyid Qutb's Thoughts on Soverity: the Notion of Democratic Participation in the Islamic Cannon", in Robbie Shilliam, ed., *International Relations and Non-Western Thought: Imperialism, Colonialism, and Investigations of Global Modernity*. Routledge: London, 87-107.
Kobayashi, Toshiaki. (2011)*Nishida Kitaro no Yuutsu* [The melancholy of Nishida Kitaro], Tokyo: Iwanami
Kobayashi, Toshiaki. (2013)*Nishida Tetsugaku wo Hiraku: <Eien no Ima> wo Megutte* [Opening Nishida's Philosophy: On the Eternal Present]. Tokyo: Iwanami.
Kosaka, Kunitsugu (2008)*Seiyo no Tetsugaku, Toyo no Shiso*, [Western Philosophy and Eastern Thought] (Tokyo: Kodansha)
Kosaka Masataka, Nishitani Keiji, Koyama Iwao, Suzuki Shigetaka (1943), *Sekaishiteki Tachiba to Nihon* [The Standpoint of World History and Japan], (Tokyo: Chuokoron)
Koyama Iwao (2001), *Sekaishi no Tetsugaku* [Philosophy of World History], (Tokyo:

Kobushishobo)

Nakano, Ryoko. (2011), "Beyond Orientalism and 'Revers Orientalism': Through the Looking Glass of Japanese Humanism", in Robbie Shilliam, ed., *International Relations and Non-Western Thought: Imperialism, Colonialism, and Investigations of Global Modernity*. Routledge: London, 125-137.

Nishida, Kitaro. (1948)"*Mu no Jikakuteki Gentei*" [The Self-Determination of Nothingness], in *Nishida Kitaro Zenshu* [Collected Works of Nishida Kitaro], No. 6. Tokyo: Iwanami.

Nishida, Kitaro. (1950a)'Sekai shinchitsujo no genri' [The principle of the new world order] in Nishida Kitaro Zenshu [Collection of Nishida Kitaro], (Tokyo: Iwanami), Vol. 12, 427-434.

Nishida, Kitaro. (1950b)'Nihonbunka no mondai' [The question of Japanese culture] in *Nishida Kitaro Zenshu* [Collection of Nishida Kitaro], (Tokyo: Iwanami), Vol. 12, 275-383.

Nishida, Kitaro. (1950c)'Tetsugaku Ronbunshu Dai 4 Hoi' [The Supplment of the Collection of Philosophical Works] in *Nishida Kitaro Zenshu* [Collection of Nishida Kitaro], (Tokyo: Iwanami), Vol. 12, 275-383.

Nishida, Kitaro. (1950e)'Kokka Riyuno Mondai' [Raison d'etre] in *Nishida Kitaro Zenshu* [Collection of Nishida Kitaro], (Tokyo: Iwanami), Vol. 10, 275-383.

Nishizuka Shunta. (2010)"*Jinsei no Hiai to "Eien no Ima" no Rekisiron no Koten: Nishida Kitaro no Shiseikan wo Megutte*" [The Sorrow of Life and the Theory of History as "Eternal Now": Reexamining Nishida Kitaro's View of Death and Life], *Shiseigaku Kenkyu* No. 13, pp. 104-126.

Ong, Graham Gerald. (2004)"Building an IR Theory with 'Japanese Characteristics': Nishida Kitaro and 'Emptiness,'" *Millennium: Journal of International Studies*, 33 (1): 35-58.

Qin Yaqing, 'Guanxi benwei yu guocheng jiangou: jiang Zhongguo linian zhiru guoji guanxi lilun' ('Relationality and Processual Construction: Bringing Chinese Ideas into International Relations Theory'), Zhongguo shehui kexue (Social Sciences in China), No. 4 (2009), pp. 5-20.

Qin, Yaqing. (2010), "Why is There no Chinese International Relations Theory?", in Acharya Amitav and Barry Buzan, eds., *Non-Western International Relations Theory: Perspectives on and Beyond Asia*, London: Routledge, 26-50.

Qin, Yaqing. (2011), "Rule, Rules, and Relations: Towards a Synthetic Approach to Governance", *Chinese Journal of International Politics*, 4, 117-145.

Shih, Chih-Yu. (2012)*Civilization, Nation and Modernity in East Asia*. London: Routledge.

Shimizu, Kosuke. (2011)"Nishida Kitaro and Japan's Interwar Foreign Policy: War Involvement and Culturalist Political Discourse," *International Relations of the Asia-Pacific*, 11 (1): pp. 157-183.

Shimizu, Kosuke (2014)'Materialising the "Non-Western": Two Stories of Japanese Philosophers on Culture and Politics in the Inter-war Period', *Cambridge Review of International Affairs*, forthcoming.

Tosa, Hiroyuki. (2009)"Obeiteki 'Fuhenshugi' no Chokoku to iu Kansei: Kyoto Gakuha Uha no Han Ajiashugi Saiko" [The Trap of Transcending Western "Universalism": Revisiting the Asianism of the Right Wing Kyoto School], *Jokyo*. 9 (9).

Williams, David. (2004)*Defending Japan's Pacific War: The Kyoto School Philosophers and Post-White Power*. London: RoutledgeCurzon.

Yan, Xuetong. (2011), *Ancient Chinese Thought, Modern Chinese Power*, Princeton: Princeton University Press.

Yoshida, Masatoshi (2011)*Kyoto Gakuha no Tetsugaku: Nishida, Miki, Tosaka wo Chushin ni*[The Philosophy of the Kyoto School: With Nishida, Miki, Tosaka], (Tokyo: Otsukishoten)

Zhao, Tingyang. (2006), "Rethinking Empire from a Chinese Concept 'All-under-Heaven (Tian-xia 天下), *Social Identities*, 12 (1), 29-41.

Zhao, Tingyang. (2012) 'All-ender-heaven and methodological relationalism', a paper presented at International Conference on Democracy, Empires and Geopolitics, Academia Sinica, Taiwan, 10–11/December/2011

INTERCULTURAL

インターカルチュラル 13 別冊

日本国際文化学会年報特別国際版

"In Search of Non-Western International Relations Theory:
The Kyoto School Revisited"

2015年3月31日発行

編　者　　日本国際文化学会［会長　白石さや］
　　　　　年報編集委員会［委員長　若林一平］

発行者　　犬塚　満
発行所　　株式会社 風 行 社
　　　　　〒101-0052　東京都千代田区神田小川町3-26-20
　　　　　Tel. & Fax. 03-6672-4001
　　　　　振替 00190-1-537252

印刷／製本　株式会社理想社

ISBN978-4-86258-093-1

©2015 Printed in Japan